A STUDY OF QI

Monkey Press is named after the Monkey King in The Journey to the West, the 16th century classical novel by Wu Chengen. Monkey blends skill, initiative and wisdom with the spirit of freedom, irreverence and mischief.

Also published by Monkey Press:
The Way of Heaven: Neijing Suwen chapters 1 and 2
The Secret Treatise of the Spiritual Orchid: Neijing Suwen chapter 8
The Seven Emotions
The Eight Extraordinary Meridians
The Extraordinary Fu
Essence Spirit Blood and Qi
The Lung
The Kidneys
Spleen and Stomach
The Heart in Ling shu chapter 8
The Liver
Heart Master Triple Heater

A STUDY OF QI

Elisabeth Rochat de la Vallée

MONKEY PRESS

AcuMedic CENTRE
101-105 CAMDEN HIGH STREET
LONDON NW1 7JN
Tel: 020 7388-6704/5783
info@acumedic.com www.acumedic.com

© Monkey Press 2006

A STUDY OF QI in classical texts

Elisabeth Rochat de la Vallée

ISBN 1 872468 28 4

www.monkeypress.net

monkey.press@virgin.net

Text Editor: Caroline Root

Production and Design: Sandra Hill

Qi Calligraphy: Qu Lei Lei

Cover image from the Mawangdui tomb archive

Printed by Biddles, Kings Lynn

CONTENTS

FOREWORD

'*Qi* itself is neither a substance nor a spirit.' This simple statement expresses some of the enigma which is *qi*. By declaring what *qi* is not it challenges us to think more deeply and precisely about what *qi* is and how we perceive, experience and use it in our lives. Likewise this new book.

Qi manifests itself in all phenomena, and is inseparable from that manifestation, so its universality ought to make it easily accessible and understood as a concept. However, even if we are practitioners of oriental medicine or of the various art forms and movement therapies which employ *qi* as an instrument or a method, we often persist with very vague notions of what we are trying to influence and direct, and we rely on the catch-all term 'energy' to explain what *qi* is.

This book is an edited transcript of two seminars given in 2004 in London by Elisabeth Rochat de la Vallée. It not only contains detailed descriptions of the various differentiated kinds of *qi*, but also a wide-ranging philosophical investigation and explanation of the origin and development of the concept of *qi* itself. It begins by looking at the historical evolution and use of the Chinese character for *qi*, and after this there are sections on how it appears in both philosophical texts such as the Zuozhuan, Zhuangzi, Mencius and the Huainanzi and in the medical texts of the Neijing and Nanjing. These give context and depth to our understanding of this ever-present but elusive activity of life.

Chinese characters are included throughout the text for clarity and precision in understanding original Chinese texts. Unless otherwise indicated, all translations from the Chinese are by Elisabeth Rochat de la Vallée. We refer to the source book Chinese Characters by Dr S.L. Wieger (Dover Language Books) where appropriate. *Qi,* in Chinese, is neither singular nor plural. Elisabeth has suggested that the plural is often a more accurate translation. *Qi* will therefore appear as singular or plural depending on the context.

'*Qi* is both everything and the specific all at the same time. It is the power of life.'

Caroline Root and Sandra Hill
June 2006

Qi

INTRODUCTION

The focus of these seminars is *qi* (氣), and as it is impossible to present a complete history of *qi* in such a short time, I have chosen passages from reliable texts which represent an interesting aspect of *qi* or illustrate the evolution of the concept of *qi*. The first part of the seminar will focus on philosophical texts, many of which originated around the second century BC. Later we will look at the medical texts of the Neijing and Nanjing.

In the centuries before the Christian era, there was a gradual development of the notion of *qi* as it grew towards our present day understanding and use. This progression was consistent with the general development of thought and laid the foundation for the building of *yin yang* and five element cosmology.

We do of course have a problem with dating Chinese texts. Some we know for sure were written before the first century BC, but it is often difficult to know exactly when. Some texts are genuinely from the third and forth centuries BC, others may be forgeries written in the first century BC! This is one of the reasons why it is impossible to make an accurate chronological history.

So this is not a history of *qi* as such, but simply a brief study of the development of the notion of *qi* as far as we can ascertain it.

THE ORIGINS OF QI

Wind

In order to understand the origin of *qi,* we must first look at the concept of wind. A character for *qi* itself does not appear in the early oracular and bronze inscriptions, or in the most ancient Chinese texts, such as The Book of Documents, Shujing, or The Book of Odes, Shijing. What we do find in the very ancient oracular inscriptions of the twelfth, thirteenth and even fourteenth centuries BC is the character for wind, and these early descriptions of wind have some of the qualities which will be later attributed to *qi.*

There are several different kinds of wind, for example the four winds and the eight winds, and each of these contributes to the growing concept of *qi.* In the beginning *qi* appears as something coming from heaven and penetrating earth. It has an influence on earth and provokes a reaction, as for instance with the *qi* that makes cold and heat, day and night, wind and rain.

Yin and yang

Later *qi* will be understood as what is behind *yin yang* (陰 陽) and this is a very important shift. We cannot speak of *qi* without speaking of *yin yang*, and we cannot speak of *yin yang* without speaking of *qi*. For instance, *yin* and *yang* appear in early texts as two of the six *qi* of heaven. They are like cold and heat, which is to say they are not only the bright, sunny side of a hill, but also the shady side. More than that they are the cold and heat which are the result of being in the sun or shade. *Yin* and *yang* will become a kind of differentiation of *qi*, as *qi* will become the influence behind any kind of manifestation. Y*in qi* will become the principle behind cold and cooling and *yang qi* will be the principle behind heat and warming.

We can see these differences evolving, and this development will be linked with changes in the weather and the passing of time, which is seen as a movement of *qi* and *yin yang*, with cooling from summer to winter and warming from winter to summer. So here *qi* is being used to codify the movement of time, and that movement is seen not only in the four seasons but also seen in the progress of each day. Many of the texts describe all this.

Internal qi

As the understanding of *qi* evolves into what is behind the appearance of things, there is the development of what we may call analogy. For instance, the same kind of *qi* making wind and tempests in nature is also seen to make anger. Therefore in early texts there is a relationship between the six *qi* of heaven and the six qualities of *qi* within a human being. These texts show the development of *qi* not only outside in nature, but also inside a human being. An example of this is seen in the Zhuangzi, where *qi* is seen not only as that which lies behind any given phenomenon, but also as the link between different phenomena presenting similar characteristics. For instance, what is behind anger and wind may also be behind all kinds of violent impulses at the beginning of something; a rising up movement, like the sunrise, or springtime.

Through this linking process we have the possibility of developing a cosmology based on *qi*, *yin yang* and the five elements. The concept of the five elements or agents, (*wu xing* 五 行), developed around the third century BC. It was not possible to develop a cosmology of correspondences before having a substantial enough notion of *qi* to make these links, which occurred around the fourth and third centuries BC.

Qi and the origin of life

At the end of the third century and the beginning of the second century BC, *qi* was linked with the origin and production of life. This is very logical, but the shift came with the understanding that *qi* is not only the power of transformation making life appear, but may also be considered as the origin of life itself. This allows us to ask what kind of relationship exists between *qi* and living beings, between *qi* and form? By 'form' we mean everything that has a specific and perfect quality; form requires substance and essences. The beginning of form is the *yin* concentration and condensation of *qi,* which allows substance to appear. When *qi* becomes *yin* and *yang* it is subject to the movements and transformations which create opposition. Within this duality of essences and *qi,* form and *qi,* the *qi* will be specific with specific qualities and no longer in totality. Therefore it may be changed, altered and even perverted, especially by the power of human nature.

So what is the relationship between *qi* and the spirits? The *qi* itself is neither a substance nor a spirit. What we may say is that *qi* manifests through phenomena, and is inseparable from that manifestation to which it gives specificity and movement. On the other hand we cannot say that *qi* is the same thing as these phenomena or beings.

When things cease to be the *qi* does not disappear, but no longer having a form, it can no longer be perceived. So we could say that it is a kind of infinite and indefinite potentiality. But 'potentiality' sounds like an abstraction, which is not the case with *qi.* It is a reality. So finally we come to the understanding that everything is *qi,* and *qi* is everything that exists.

Therefore heaven and earth and all that is between them, everything that may envelope them and all the beings and phenomena existing between them, are just specific manifestations of *qi* which exist for a while. If it is an emotion it is for today. If it is a mountain it is for longer. Eventually we have the vision that everything is *qi*, right up to the point that the essences themselves are just a concentration of *qi*.

The Chinese also have a passion for unity, and through their vision of *qi* found the unity of all things. Within this vision, my *qi* is not exactly my own, it is mine because it is my life at the moment. And it is the same thing with my spirits. My spirits are not specifically my own, they are mine because they are effective in my life at this moment. If my life comes to an end, the spirits and the *qi* will not disappear but they will be something or somewhere else. They will continue to participate in the infinite and unlimited movement of life. This is not an adequate description because we are deficient in language to speak of what lies behind the appearance of living beings. But *qi* is at that level; it is at the level of the origin of all manifestation of life. So the colour, the sound and the smell of a specific being are all a matter of *qi*.

At the same time, we also have the idea of *qi* as the *yang* side in all *yin yang* relationships, such as blood and *qi*, essences and *qi*, body form and *qi*. So the question is whether the *qi* are able to be the natural order of life on their own or do we need to add something? This 'added something' has been called by different names according to the era and the school of thought: the Dao, the Li, the principles of the Confucian school, or the *shen* (神). There are several approaches in later texts, but essentially the feeling is that the *qi* follow 'guidance' from heaven in some way. But we have to be careful here, because even if the *qi* are in relationship with something giving guidance, there is no duality. Ultimate reality is always the merging of opposites in unity. We have to be very clear about this because it is an error that is sometimes made in the west.

USES OF QI

The cosmology which we see in Chinese medicine and in Daoism is based on *qi*, *yin yang* and *wu xing* (the five elements/agents). A rich understanding of the notion of *qi* is necessary to allow this cosmology to exist and to function with all its correspondences. If *qi* was just cold or heat for example, it would not be possible to have a foundation for this complex cosmology. Obviously the diversity and richness of the concept of *qi* was not present in Chinese thinking before the third century BC, there was no trace of it then, and therefore no possibility of such connections being made in order to establish a cosmology.

If you open a good Chinese dictionary you may find under *qi* several meanings which are an expression of the various historical uses of *qi*. For instance, there can be a state of undifferentiated totality in which everything is *qi*. It can be the life-giving principle, original *qi*, or the components of the constituent agent of all which exists. You can also have the idea of the life force and activity in any organism or phenomenon, the vigour of motion, energy, the animating forces of the universe. *Qi* is also used for more observable things, for instance breath, steam, gas or vapour. All of these are found in this character.

Qi gives movement, change and transformation to the various expressions of life, and allows the manifestation of specific qualities and aspects. For instance, in nature it is air, but it is also the state of nature itself, the weather and the atmosphere. It is each of the four seasons, and each of the 24 periods of 15 days which form the solar year. The 24 periods of the year are called *jie qi* (節 氣). *Qi* is also used to express any amount of time.

In the organism *qi* can be used to mean breathing, exhalation, or any kind of utterance. It can also describe colour and appearance, and is the manner, attitude, bearing and expression of the container. For example, the expression which I have on my face is the result of *qi*. My demeanour and body language are all a manifestation of *qi*, as are my temper, temperament and emotions. 'Spleen *qi*' (*pi qi* 脾 氣) is a popular expression in Chinese for the mood of the day, and to be in a bad mood is to have bad spleen *qi*. Of course *qi* is also used for the *yang* expression of anger, to make *qi* is to be angry, but it is also used for a state of mind, and the natural movement or disposition of the heart. So it is used for the vital forces, not only of the body with the strength of the constitution, but also for the force of the mind. Thus the intelligence, or will power of any being is also *qi*. To be animated or spirited is due to *qi*, and it is used for everything that can be expressed. When looking at calligraphy, you may say there is *qi* within the characters. This is something that is felt. The idea of *qi* lies behind all kinds of manifestation, and at the same time it is the life-giving force.

This understanding of *qi*, and our ability to perceive it, lies behind all the various methods of diagnosis used in Chinese medicine, the movement and quality of *qi* being an expression of what lies beneath.

THE CHARACTER FOR QI

The character *qi* (氣) does not appear in any archaic inscriptions or even in the earliest Chinese written texts. The outer part (气) is found in old texts and in oracular inscriptions where it means to ask or to pray for. It is something that is coming from below and rising up. So the general meaning in ancient times was to make a ritual prayer.

By the time of the Shuowen Jiezi, the etymological dictionary published at the beginning of the second century AD upon which Wieger's 'Chinese Characters' is based, a lot of the original forms of writing had been lost, along with the primitive meanings. For instance, in trying to explain this character (气), the writers of the Shuowen Jiezi did not know that the primitive meaning was to pray, to offer a prayer, or to demand something. So the analysis of this character (气) is of ascending vapour forming clouds. The movement is nearly the same. Something ascends from below and accumulates above with a kind of purpose. This idea is developed in the complete form of the character *qi* (氣). The ascending vapours now come from the cooking of grain, because inside the character for *qi* there is a bursting grain (米).

In this character for *qi* we can see a relationship between the grain boiling and bursting, and making something appear in the form of a vapour with the strength to lift up the lid of the saucepan. So we need to include in the meaning the idea of a kind of heat and force which makes things function. Little by little the character *qi* was charged with all these meanings.

THE CHARACTER FOR WIND

The character for wind, *feng* (風), has some similarity with the character for *qi* in the movement of the air or vapour represented by the outside strokes (几). Inside there is the image of an insect or little worm (虫). This is a general character used for a lot of little creatures. When you have one you have ten thousand! This suggests that wind is present because all these insects are moving and perhaps the wind is able to awaken their metamorphosis and put them in motion, especially in the springtime. This is a nice image of life in all its transformations (*sheng hua* 生 化). In spring in the south of China or Taiwan there is a sudden rainy season. Then one day the sun shines and during the evening a lot of insects appear. First they fly, then they become little worms and after that they disappear, all in three days or so. So when the Chinese speak of 'the rain of insects' they are speaking of observed reality. It is not just a poetic image.

So when we look at the character for wind (風), it is not only that there is an insect in the wind, it is a lot more than that. As is said in the Shuowen Jiezi, it is the wind which makes the insects appear and transform. This is a very old idea of the wind being the power able to make life appear in insects and vegetation, and to give them the ability to be transformed. With insects it is metamorphosis and with grains it is the ability to grow and ripen. Certainly, back in the ancient times of the twelfth, thirteenth or fourteenth centuries BC, the wind appears to have been considered this kind of life-giving and transformative power; the breaths sent by heaven to awaken life within the earth.

The character for phoenix (鳳) is similar to that for the wind, and has the same pronunciation, *feng*. This is not by chance. The ancient character for wind represented a phoenix with a proud and fierce bearing. The phoenix was one of the assistants of the Supreme Being, the Great Ancestor, in charge of the four winds and the four territories organized around the centre where the reigning power was established. This cosmology was the foundation of the Shang-Yin dynasty.

Even at this very remote period in time there was a notion of different winds. A wind from the south was not the same as a wind from the north or the east. Wind was also considered a messenger of the Supreme Being, bringing life, transformation and fertility, all that is necessary for the development of life. Wind came from heaven and had an action on earth, for instance on insects or on vegetation. Clearly this is a basis for the beginning of the notion of *qi*. A character for *qi* had not yet appeared with a fixed meaning, but the wind and its effects were certainly a way of perceiving the vital forces.

QI IN PHILOSOPHICAL TEXTS

CHUNQIU ZUOZHUAN

We will begin with the Chunqiu Zuozhuan, the commentary of Mr Zuo on the historical chronicle called the Spring and Autumn Annals. In fact it is not certain that it is a commentary on the Spring and Autumn Annals at all, but it is probably a text from sometime between the first and third centuries BC, with some rectification made in the first century BC. It might even be a forgery from the first century, but if it is it is a good one because we cannot decide! If it is a forgery, it is an attempt to reinstate the way of thinking of previous centuries.

The book is the year by year presentation of the succession of the Dukes of the kingdom of Lu from the eighth to the fifth centuries BC. Lu was the home state of Confucius and this is the reason why the treatise is said to be written by Confucius. Certainly he knew the basic writings. The following is a text of Duke Zhao or Zhao Gong, in the first year:

'Heaven has six *qi* (*liu qi* 六 氣) which descending generate five tastes (*wu wei* 五 味), issue as five colours, are evidenced by five sounds, and in excess they generate six diseases. The six *qi* are

> *yin* and *yang*, wind and rain, darkness and light (*yin yang feng yu hui ming* 陰 陽 風 雨 晦 明). They divide to make the four seasons (*si shi* 四 時) in sequence, make the five rhythms (*wu jie* 五 節), and in excess bring about calamities.'

After this the text continues:

> 'From *yin* in excess, cold diseases. From *yang* in excess, hot diseases. From wind in excess, diseases of the extremities. From rain in excess, diseases of the stomach. From darkness in excess, diseases of delusions. From light in excess, diseases of the heart.'

Here *yin* and *yang* are associated with cold, felt in the shade, and heat, felt in sunshine, and express the possibility of cold and heat generating illness inside the body. This is one of the first major texts on the influence of *qi*, and here for the first time the *qi* are described as coming from heaven. The three pairs or couples of *qi* from heaven result in the appearance on earth of the five tastes, the five colours and the five sounds; six being related to heaven and five to earth. The six *qi* of heaven appear inside the earthly beings by giving them specific tastes, colours or sounds.

IN PHILOSOPHICAL TEXTS · 15

IN PHILOSOPHICAL TEXTS · 15

Systems of five qi and six qi

There are several points to note about this. First of all we are not within the cosmology of the five elements here. The series of five existed in China from a very early time, but it is not because this series existed that we later had a cosmology based on the five elements. We are probably more used to five, as an odd number, being linked with heaven and *yang,* and six, as an even number, with earth and *yin.* But at this time during the fifth and fourth centuries BC, six was more likely to be the number for heaven, so here there are six *qi* in heaven, three pairs of opposites, which are the origin of a reaction by and on earth. It is after the second century BC that odd numbers are linked to heaven and even numbers to earth. Five was then linked with heaven.

So why in medicine do we have two series of atmospheric influences coming from outside, one ruled by five and one by six? The reason is because we have two systems. There is the remainder of the *liu qi* (六 氣) system, the six *qi* of heaven, and there is the system by five which came afterwards, with the five *qi* corresponding to the five elements and five influences coming from heaven.

In this text, the six *qi* generate something on earth, and not only on earth but in human beings too. And of course, human beings generate the six kinds of illnesses. These illnesses and calamities in nature exist because there is excess. So we have the idea of the correct and perverse *qi*, although it is not yet called 'perverse', just excess. This is *qi* which does not follow the good rhythm or natural movement of life, and which therefore invades the earth or the body like an enemy. The character translated as 'excess' is *yin* (淫), meaning irregular or deregulated; it is also found in medical books. It is often used for irregular *qi* coming from outside, and in the vocabulary of medicine we have the six *yin*, wind, cold, heat, dryness, dampness and fire. It is a character often used with the idea of licentiousness, but also of invading in order to put in the wrong direction. For instance, if you are with friends and they are involved in debauched behaviour, little by little you will be influenced by their excess. They will be too strong for you to remain correct. So this *qi* is too strong not to affect the normal way of life. Life cannot retain its correct pattern, and therefore there are calamities on earth, or illnesses in the body. These six *qi*, which result on earth in various series of five, are also the basis for the four seasons. They are the regular alternation of weather and time, which makes the rhythm of the seasons. They are *yin* and *yang* or cold and heat, progressing throughout the year to make the seasons, wind and rain creating the weather, and light and dark bringing the alternation of day and night.

The five rhythms and the regulation of qi

These rhythms are the *jie* (節), which etymologically means the knots in bamboo. In its structure bamboo expresses the alternation of *yin* and *yang*, emptiness and fullness, activity and rest, display and concentration. In the Shuo Wen Jiezi the explanation of the character *jie* is to take a measured amount of rice in a pot. The cooking pot containing boiled white rice (*bai* 白) and the spoon (*bi* 匕) are depicted in the character along with the idea of a measure, with the bamboo radical up above (竹). So the meaning is to be able to have a regular measurement, similar to that of the articulations on a bamboo shoot. *Jie* (節) is therefore linked with *qi* because it is important for *qi* to have an even measure, and not to be in excess or deficiency. But at the same time *jie* contains ideas of alternation and rhythm. *Qi* is always *yin* and *yang* passing from cold to heat, concentration to dispersion.

The five rhythms (*wu jie* 五 節) give the solar year an organization by five. The eight *jie*, or eight rhythms of the year are the two solstices, the two equinoxes and the four beginnings of each season. They are the days of the year when there is a kind of 'knot' regulating all the movement of *qi*. And we have seen that the 24 periods of the year are called *jie qi* (節 氣).

In this text from the Chunqiu Zuozhuan, we can see that there is a lot of information coming from a more ancient cosmology, but it is not quite the same as the more evolved notion of *qi* or the five elements, or even *yin yang.* In this text *yin yang* is not yet the blueprint for all coupled concepts. It represents one among several. Here *yin* represents the cool of the shadows and *yang* the heat of the sun. These ideas will gradually evolve into an expression of *qi* itself, but that will be later.

Staying with the Zuozhuan I will take another text from the same chapter, Duke Zhao's first year. It says:

'The sage respects the four moments of time.'

In Chinese this is '*jun zi you si shi* (君 子 有 四 時)'. *Jun zi* (君 子) is the name given to a sage or a gentleman. *You* (有) is to have, *si* (四) is four and *shi* (時) is a moment of time, or more specifically an hour, day or season of a year. The phrase *si shi* (四 時) usually means the four seasons, but with Chinese the translation always has to be made according to the context. In this text it does not refer to the four seasons but to the four divisions of the day.

'In the morning he holds an audience. During the day he collects information. In the evening he writes down the orders. During the night he rests.'

An audience would involve listening to people

seeking arbitration or judgement. This takes place in the morning because at dawn after the rest of the night we are in a more balanced state, and is reflected in medicine with the practice of taking the pulse at dawn when the *qi* is balanced. We rest at night in order to let the *qi* come back to a more normal movement and to let the *yin* restore the quietness and good rhythm of that movement. The prince normally held his audience at dawn. This was explained in the Book of Rites, one of the Five Classics written around the second century BC, as being because at dawn there was a perfect state of balance. Taking advantage of the rest of the night and not yet being in disorder caused by the agitation of the day. This is why when you want to take someone's pulses away from the specific circumstances created by their daily activity, you take them at dawn.

During the day the sage collects all the necessary information. As a wise and powerful man he does not go to work in a field and come home at night exhausted. He needs to gather information in order to find the right way to govern, which is the way of the leader. To be a leader is to find a centre which has a deep root in the reality of life. In the evening when he has collected information and centered himself within the cosmos, then he can take decisions. At night, he rests. What follows is more interesting:

'Doing that he is able to regulate the diffusion of

his *qi* (*jie xuan qi qi* (節 宣 其 氣).'

We have looked at the character *jie* (節) to regulate. *Xuan* (宣) is familiar in Chinese physiology associated with the lung, and is the idea of disseminating, spreading out everywhere, but following a good rhythm in doing so. The sage regulates the diffusion of his *qi*. It continues:

'Acting in such a way that the *qi* will not block or stagnate.'

We find this in a lot of other texts, that the great problem with *qi,* in nature as well as in the human body, is blockage from stagnation. Water provides a good image of this. Water must circulate normally, not to stagnate or block. If it blocks or stagnates then it becomes unhealthy. In the body it is the same thing. The problem is how to avoid an excess of *qi* or an invasion of *qi*, which may disturb our own *qi*. Through our own behaviour we have to make sure that *qi* is diffused regularly without any blockage or stagnation. Blockage or stagnation will lead to 'physical exhaustion, lack of clarity in the heart/mind, and confusion in thoughts and thinking'.

Therefore, if you are wise enough you can understand something about the rhythms of nature and *qi*, and know that the regulation of *qi* is not only a question of weather but also of good health. And although human beings may be subject to invasion due to some kind of excess in the surrounding *qi*, they can also take advantage of their human ability to keep a natural rhythm of *qi* inside themselves. Following the four movements of time and the rhythms of each day, allows the body and heart/mind (*xin* 心) to be in perfect condition with strength of body and clarity of mind.

So this is not only a question of the *qi* within an individual, but of how it can be regulated by means of individual behaviour. This idea was developed more and more through the centuries BC, until finally the individual is seen as ultimately responsible for every kind of disorder. This is something which we find in chapter 55 of the Daodejing: 'The heart puts *qi* into action as envoy (*xin shi qi* 心 使 氣)'. In the context of Laozi chapter 55, the heart is making the *qi* too active and the result is violence. But nevertheless this shows that the heart is considered to be responsible for putting the *qi* into movement.

THE ART OF WAR

We find this idea everywhere, for example in the Zunzi (The Art of War) chapter 7:

'A whole army may be deprived of its morale

(its *qi);* a general may be deprived of his heart
(his mind, his fortitude). In the morning, the *qi*
is eager, at noon, it flags; by evening it is home
sick. Thus the expert in the military avoids [the
enemy] when its *qi* is eager, but attacks when it is
flagging or home sick. This is to control the *qi.*'

Here we have a passage about the morale of soldiers,
but what is usually translated as morale is in fact *qi*. It
is about the *qi* of the soldiers according to the various
times of day. For example, in the early morning at dawn
the soldiers are full of *qi*, but during the day there is a
slowing down of this impetuosity, and when the evening
comes the soldiers sink back to their home place, so
there is a diminution of their *qi*, or a kind of stagnation
if you like. In a treatise on the art of war this would
be an indication of when to attack the enemy army;
you attack them in the evening, never at dawn. But of
course you have to pay attention to the *qi* of your own
soldiers. This shows that in a text completely different
from the Laozi there is the same idea of *qi*, the rhythm
of the *qi* inside a person, and the way to manage that.

THE SIX QI

In the text of the 25th year of Duke Zhao from the
Chunqiu Zuozhuan, there is a passage that directly

relates the six *qi* of heaven to what happens inside a human being at the level of their inner disposition and tendencies. It reads:

'In mankind the likes and dislikes, elation and anger (*xi nu* 喜 怒), sorrow and joy (*ai le* 哀 樂), are generated from the six *qi*. Therefore, take care to model yourself on appropriate categories in order to control the six inclinations or wills (*liu zhi* 六 志).'

Here again we can see the relationship between atmospheric conditions and feelings in human beings. In medicine we often have five expressions of will and seven emotions, each with the symbolic values of five and seven as they were in the period of the expansion of medical thinking. But at the time of this text there were six kinds of emotions or inner dispositions, usually seen in three pairs of opposites, for example elation and anger. Here the six *qi* are not only the six *qi* of the surrounding environment, but also six kinds of movement, or modes of activity, which are inside a person and generated by them. In medical thinking they are generated by the five *zang*. This gives rise to the idea that the *qi* must be guided. We must model our conduct on a particular pattern in order to have well circulating *qi*, moving with good timing and rhythm. This is why the text says that you must take care to model yourself on the 'appropriate categories'. But what are the appropriate categories? They are a kind of pattern of conduct, for instance what to eat, what kind of music to listen to, how to behave, and what rites and rituals to perform. Rituals are always, according to the traditional Chinese view, the way to model oneself on nature. One of the best ways in ancient times to understand the movement of *qi* in nature and natural behaviour was through ritual and rite. By following the rites which teach you how to behave, what and when to eat, how to dress, what kind of music to listen to and so on, you regulate the six *qi* inside yourself. Another passage from the Duke Zhao's 25th year says:

> 'Ritual (*li* 禮) is the standard (*jing* 經) of heaven, the principle (*yi* 義) of earth, and the conduct (*xing* 行) of man. Heaven and earth have their standards and men take these for their pattern, with the light of heaven as model and the generation of earth as basis, the six *qi* are generated using the five processes (*wu xing* 五行). The *qi* become the five tastes, issue as the five colours, and are proclaimed as the five sounds.'

Therefore through ritual we know how to dress in the appropriate colours, how to eat the appropriate grains and meats and so on. We regulate our internal *qi*, and thus regulate our inner disposition and emotions. In this way we naturally control or govern the six wills (*liu zhi* 六 志). *Zhi* is usually translated in medical texts as will, or will power, but in earlier texts it was simply an inclination or propensity. It is normal to like or dislike certain things, but it must be an appropriate and controlled response, not an excessive reaction. If your *qi* is in good order you will act appropriately with all you own tendencies and propensities, but if your *qi* is in disorder then your reactions and emotions will also be out of control. Harmony, *he* (和), is always composed and the result of several things, or of everything coming together.

In another text from the 20th year of Duke Zhao, there is the story of a prince who is behaving badly. The head of the kitchen, not the chef, but a high ranking official, asks why the prince is behaving so badly. He says that there are three people responsible. As head of the kitchen, he is responsible for whatever enters the prince by mouth, the master of music is responsible for what enters by the ear, and another high official is responsible for what the prince's eyes see.

'The tastes guide (*xing* 行) the *qi*, the *qi* makes the will (*zhi* 志) solid (*shi* 實), the will fixes speech (the word) (*yan* 言).'

This is a very old idea that can be found in many other texts, for example the Guoyu, the Speech of the

Kingdoms, a very ancient text, perhaps from the end of the fifth century BC. It says:

'The mouth draws in taste and the ear sounds. Sounds and tastes generate *qi*. The *qi* in the mouth becomes speech and in the eyes becomes light (*ming* 明, good vision).'

This is a similar idea that everything that penetrates the body with or without a form, for instance tastes proceeding through the mouth and stomach and sounds entering the ear, produce and pervade the *qi* inside the individual. Because of that *qi* the person is able to speak, see and whatever else is done.

Food and qi

Coming back to the previous text of Duke Zhao's 20th year about the kitchen master, the three sentences are very interesting. The text says that the tastes activate and guide the *qi*. There is a very strong and primitive link between food and *qi*. It is vitally important to eat carefully because it is not only a question of good health but a question of good *qi* and its regulation. The *qi* is able to make the will solid, and the will is the able to direct and form the inner disposition. It is your inner disposition that determines what you say. For a prince, it is important to give orders when it is appropriate. To do that he has to have a firm and solid direction in his mind, and to achieve that his *qi* must be well regulated by appropriate and well balanced food. A little bit later in the text the prince asks:

> "'Are harmony and identity different?" Yanzi answered, "They are. Harmony may be illustrated by broth. You have water and fire, vinegar, pickle, salt and plums, with which to cook fish. It is made to boil by the firewood, and then the cook mixes the ingredients, harmoniously equalizing whatever is in excess. Then the master eats it, and his heart/mind is made equable."' (Based on the translation by Fung Yu-lan)

So here the chef is creating harmony in the broth, just as one composes a recipe. All the tastes must be present, but in the right proportions so that one is not dominant. One taste can prevail according to the season, for example, it is normal that the broth would be a little bit sour during the springtime, but not too much so. All this is a metaphor for the balance of the emotions. The emotional balance or equilibrium of the mind is not a stable thing, it is always changing and evolving according to the individual life, the season, the circumstances and so on, but it must always remain in the right proportion and balance. *Ping* (平) is to make equable, to put in balance, with the idea of a peaceful balance.

The texts ends by saying that the ancient kings, who were very wise, combined the five tastes and tuned the five sounds in order to put the heart in balance and to govern perfectly.

All this is a question of *qi*. The correct rhythm will always be achieved through the regulation of *qi*. There are many texts which show this, one of which is a very important book written around the middle of the third century BC, the Lüshi Chunqiu, the Spring and Autumn Annals of Lü Buwei. In the last chapter of this book it says:

'Grains, when they are harvested at the right time, have a pleasant smell and a sweet taste. They give the *qi* splendour. During the period of the one hundred days of this good grain, another result is that one will have acute and accurate sight and hearing, and clarity and wisdom in the heart and mind. The four limbs will be strong and firm. Pernicious *qi* will not enter you, so your body will not have any serious disease. The Yellow Emperor said: "If something is not regular and correct in the four seasons, start by regulating the five grains."'

MENCIUS

This text from the end of the fourth century BC is a kind of parable about Ox Mountain.

'There was a time when the trees were luxuriant on Ox Mountain, but as it is on the outskirts of a great metropolis, the trees are constantly lopped by axes. Is it any wonder that they are no longer fine? With the respite they get in the day and night, and the moistening by the rain and dew, there is certainly no lack of new shoots coming out, but the cattle and sheep come to graze upon the mountain. This is why it is as bald as it is. People, seeing only its baldness, tend to think that it never had any trees. But can that possibly be the nature of a mountain? Can what is in man be complete lacking in moral inclination? A man's letting go of his true heart is like the case of the trees and the axes. When the trees are lopped day after day, is it any wonder that they are no longer fine? If, in spite of the respite a man gets in the day and night and the effect of the dawn's *qi* on him, scarcely any of his likes and dislikes resemble those of other men, it is because what he does in the course of the day once again dissipates what he has gained. If this dissipation happens repeatedly, then the healing influence of the night *qi* will no longer be able to preserve what was originally in him, and when that happens the man is not far removed from an animal.' (Mencius Book V1, part A, paragraph 8 translated by D.C. Lau. In certain other editions of Mencius, you will find this passage in chapter 11 section 8.)

What is translated as the 'healing influence of the air in the night' or 'the healing influence of the night *qi* is simply *ye qi*, night *qi*. Furthermore, what is translated by 'the effect of the morning air' is the dawn *qi*', the *qi* at the beginning of the day. At dawn the *qi* is in a natural state of balance, and because of this it is quiet. Because it is quiet you have clarity of mind. Because you have clarity of mind, as is said in Daoist texts such as Zhuangzi chapter 15, you are able to be in the Way. Or in a Confucian text you may say one is able to see clearly what is good and what is bad.

The character for dawn used in this text is the character *dan* (旦) which represents the growing of the sun. The sun is seen rising above the horizon. This *dan* is well known, but dawn is also expressed by the phrase *ping dan* (平旦): dawn as a time when everything is in balance.

Continuing with another text from Mencius we can begin to consider *qi* related to the will and the heart. This famous text is from Book 11, part A, paragraph

2, or Book 11 section 2 according to the numbering system.

'I wonder if you could tell me something about the heart that cannot be stirred (*bu dong xin* 不動心), in your case and in Gaozi's case?'

'According to Gaozi, "If you fail to understand words (*yan* 言) do not worry about this in your heart (*xin* 心); and if you fail to understand in your heart, do not seek satisfaction in your *qi* (氣)." It is right that one should not seek satisfaction in one's *qi* when one fails to understand it in one's heart. But it is wrong to say that one should not worry about it in one's heart when one fails to understand words. The will (*zhi* 志) is commander over the *qi* (*qi zhi shi* 氣 之 師) while the *qi* is that which fills the body (*ti zhi chong* 體 之 充). Where the will arrives, there the *qi* halts. Hence it is said, "take hold of your will and do not abuse your *qi*"'.

'As you have already said that where the will arrives there the *qi* halts, what is the point of going on to say, "take hold of your will and do not abuse your *qi*"?'

'The will, when blocked, moves the *qi* (*dong xin* 動心). On the other hand, the *qi*, when blocked, also moves the will (*dong zhi* 動志). Now stumbling and hurrying affect the *qi*, yet in fact palpitations of the heart are produced.'

'May I ask what your strong points are?'

'I have an insight into words. I am good at cultivating my "flood-like *qi*" (*hao ran zhi qi* 浩 然 之 氣).

'May I ask what this "flood-like *qi*" is?'

'It is difficult to explain. This is a *qi* which is, in the highest degree, vast and unyielding. Nourish it with integrity (*zhi yang* 直 養) and place no obstacle in its path and it will fill the space between Heaven and Earth. It is a *qi* which unites rightness (*yi* 義) and the Way (*dao* 道). Deprive it of these and it will starve. It is born of accumulated rightness and cannot be appropriated by anyone through a sporadic show of rightness. Whenever one acts in a way that falls below the standard set in one's heart, it will starve. Hence I said Gaozi never understood rightness because he looked upon it as external.' (Based on D.C. Lau's translation)

In this passage from Mencius the *qi* is the sensitivity and activity of our innermost nature. But this richness, this power within, needs regulation, which is given here by the will.

This text is one of the most important about *qi* in ancient classical Chinese. It says several things. First, that there is a relationship between the *qi* within which makes life, and the state of mind and the balance of their heart. Here we have what Mencius called the heart that cannot be stirred. This is a heart which is not moved, which means not agitated or disturbed. This is nothing to do with the beating of the heart. I say this because in Chinese the same character *dong* (動) is also used for the beating of the heart.

All sorts of movements can put your heart out of balance. But how does that happen? There are several ways. We understand that *qi* is always at risk of disturbing the heart. The problem is that the same *qi* which is the troublemaker is also the life-maker. The same *qi* is both the power of your life and the disturber of your life.

The first question is how to maintain an unstirred heart. The answer is 'if you fail to understand words, do not worry about this in your heart'. This means that if there is something which you are unable to express clearly, do not try to understand it by thinking, because if you are unable to express it clearly and accurately, the effort of thinking will only result in an increase in the uncertainty and confusion. When everything is functioning well and everything you see and receive is transformed well, it gives clarity to your heart and mind, which is expressed through clear speech. If your speech is not clear, it is because there is something wrong in the *qi*. If you attempt to make clarity with the heart/mind you will not succeed and will only increase the confusion. For example, if I have to make a decision about which road to take it may be clear at once, but if it is not I may have to think about it. But the fact is that this kind of thinking is dangerous, because if I were able to know, I would have had a clear idea straight away. To try to remember can really increase the confusion. Asking your instinct to tell you what to do is the same thing. It will be wrong because your internal *qi* is not well regulated and it cannot indicate the right way forward.

Qi and the will

When the heart is in perfect balance and all the movements of *qi* are well regulated, then thinking is clear. This is the reason why Mencius goes on to discuss the relationship between the *qi* and the will or intent (*zhi* 志), the inner orientation of the mind. The relationship between them concerns the guidance given by the *zhi* to the *qi*.

As we saw earlier, the *qi* is generally understood as an unlimited vital force, but not exactly as the guide or ruler of life. Life is a spontaneous activity of the *qi*, but there is also something which makes this activity regular as well as spontaneous. It is this that we have to embody in ourselves as human beings, and which is called 'Heaven' or the 'Way'.

This can be seen in the well known medical classical text, the beginning of Lingshu chapter 8:

'Heaven in me is virtue (*tian zhi zai wo zhe de ye* 天 之 在 我 者 德 也), Earth in me is *qi* (*di zhi zai wo zhe qi ye* 地 之 在 我 者 氣 也).'

Why is the *qi* related to earth? It is because *qi* represents all the possibilities of the expression of life appearing on earth, and in the human body it is the multiplicity of what makes our life. But before the *qi* there is the virtue (*de* 德), the uprightness of the movement coming from heaven. (Cf The Heart in Lingshu Chapter 8, Monkey Press 2004)

Here we have a sequential relationship between the *qi* and the will. The will, or intent, guides the *qi* through the inner orientation coming from the heart. If this is so everything will be in order. If one cultivates oneself by all the means available, such as education or the rituals of the Confucian school, the will is in front and the *qi* will follow. There is an activation of the *qi*. But any kind of excess or lack of regulation in the movement of *qi* will lead to a disturbance in the peaceful rhythm of the heart or the balance of the mind, which in Chinese is the same thing.

Flood-like qi

The description of 'flood-like *qi*' (*hao ran zhi qi* 浩 然 之 氣) in the text from Mencius is a very famous phrase. *Hao* (浩) is a meeting of something which is pervasive or flowing everywhere. It has the water radical on the left side. *Ran* (然), with the fire radical beneath, is something natural, something that goes by itself. There is nothing artificial about it. It is a kind of sea which is at ease. In this sentence we have the feeling of *qi* which is extending everywhere quite naturally, and there is a sense of the unlimited power and presence of that *qi* in every living being. Mencius himself said it is difficult to describe and explain this. This kind of *qi* is extremely powerful and vigorous, and when it is maintained and sustained with uprightness and rectitude, then it fills everywhere between heaven and earth. This is also the beginning of a kind of cosmic consciousness, with the *qi* within and the *qi* without being the same. The internal *qi*, if maintained correctly, is unlimited. It allows participation in the cosmic life. The *qi* is unlimited, inexhaustible if we guide it correctly, and do not pervert it by inappropriate will and desire. These ideas are developed later on in Mencius.

In the Doctrine of the Mean (Zhongyong) there is a final achievement of its expression in the man who is a sage and able to embody this *qi*. Not only is he well centred but he is also the centre of heaven, earth and the whole universe. Through our *qi* we have to develop interaction with heaven and earth, leading to the theory expounded in the second century BC of the three powers: heaven, earth and mankind. When we speak of the three powers we have to understand that human beings have power, together with heaven and earth, to balance that which exists in themselves, in nature and also in the cosmos.

QI AND FORM

In the Zuozhuan, in Duke Zhuang's 14th year, there is a story about some people who saw two serpents fighting at the gate of the city:

'Before this, two serpents one inside and one outside, had fought together at the southern gate of the capital, till the inside one was killed. It was six years after this when Duke Li entered. The Duke (of Lao) heard of the circumstances and asked Shin Seu saying, "Has Tuh's restoration come from that supernatural appearance?" The answer was, "When men are full of fear, the breath *(qi)* as it were, blazes up, and brings such things. Monsters and monstrous events take their rise from men. If men afford no cause for them, they do not arise of themselves. When men abandon the constant course (of virtue), then monstrosities appear. Therefore it is that there are monsters and monstrous events.' [Based on the translation by James Legge]

The answer is very interesting. It says that when a man is fearful, the *qi* that is exhaled is like a flame that attracts something. This attraction comes from the man himself. The explanation is that when a man has something in his heart, the *qi* emanating from him is almost in a physical form. It carries something of the disposition of the heart and the feeling of the man, and this *qi* is given form. Remember that in medicine *qi* always precedes the taking of a form. *Qi* creates the form to be taken.

Qi has diverse qualities and balances, but must always be present to make a form appear, even if the form is very subtle, like changing clouds. A feeling in the heart of the people produced the *qi* referred to in the passage from Duke Zhuang's 14th year, and in this case the form taken had the image of two struggling snakes. So these kinds of apparitions can have their origin in human beings. This is very interesting in such an old text, and later it will become more developed. As human beings we not only receive *qi* but we release *qi*, through breathing and through being who we are and what we feel.

The *qi* released by human beings has an effect on

the balance between heaven and earth. When there is something wrong in the behaviour of an individual, strange apparitions and bizarre phenomena start to appear. This theory flourished during the Han Dynasty which was roughly 200 BC - 200 AD. Generally speaking there are two layers of strange phenomena. There is a kind of lower level, for instance the raining of frogs, which is a way for nature or heaven to give a warning that there is something wrong and it must be rectified. The second level occurs if no correction is made, and then there will be real calamities.

HUAINANZI AND THE GENERATION OF QI

Question: What is it that holds the qi in place? Do the forces which produce the qi have to be held in place?

It is difficult to speak of the generation of *qi*. There are several texts with several different approaches. It is more that *qi* is everywhere and everything. There is a text in the Huainanzi chapter 7 that says at first there is a kind of undifferentiated one-ness. There is *qi*, but we cannot see anything, it is not yet *yin* or *yang*, and there is no creation:

'Of antiquity (*gu* 古), before heaven and earth even existed, there were only images (*xiang* 像)

without forms (*wu xing* 無 形), profound, opaque,
vast, immobile, impalpable and still. There was
a haziness, infinite, unfathomable, abysmal, to
which no one knew the door (*men* 門).'

If the universe, the unlimited cosmos, is seen as
qi we must also look at the cosmos as having a self-
producing and self-regulating role. It is not that we
create *qi* or that *qi* is created, but that there is the
manifestation of life through the *qi* and the forms which
the *qi* enables. So it is difficult to speak of a creation of
qi because in a way the *qi* is already here. It has always
been here, before time and space, and through what
is here we may perceive the differentiations making
time and space, heaven and earth and all living beings.
These are all inside the wholeness and the oneness.
Nothing can really be exterior. This implies that there is
no creative process as we know it, because if there is a
creative process there is a schism between creator and
creation, and that does not exist in the Chinese mind.
This is of course the basis of the *dao*, and *qi* is just the
result of making the multiplicity appear through *yin
yang* and through heaven and earth.

At the beginning of Huainanzi chapter 3 (from the
beginning of the second century BC) there is a great
text that fits with this inquiry:

'When heaven and earth were not yet formed (*wei*

xing 未 形) it was amorphous, vague, a blank, a blur. Before the primal beginning (*tai shi* 太始) the Way (*dao* 道) began in the tenuous and transparent. The tenuous and the transparent generated space and time (*yu zhou* 宇 宙). Space and time generated the *qi*. There was a dividing line (*ya yin* 涯 垠) in the *qi*. The clear and soaring spread out to become heaven, the heavy and muddy (unclear) congealed to become earth. The concentration of subtle is easy. The concretion of the heavy and muddy is difficult.' [Based on a translation by John S. Mayor]

The whole of this chapter deals with *qi*, *yin yang* and so on. Therefore this is one of the first texts on what we may call cosmogenesis. It is a very beautiful text, but difficult to translate.

In Huainanzi chapter 3 we are introduced to the concept of original *qi*, which is the starting point for the process of the production of a specific life. Original *qi* is just the beginning of differentiated life. We have to understand this not chronologically, but as a constant movement of appearing and disappearing related to the forces of heaven and earth.

At the beginning of the Huainanzi chapter 7 it says that the finest and most essential *qi* makes human beings and the less refined *qi* makes animals:

'The coarse *qi* (*fan qi* 煩 氣) made inferior animals (*chong* 蟲), and the finest *qi* (*jing qi* 精 氣) made humans.'

I want to look briefly at another text from near the end of Huainanzi chapter 1. It is a kind of continuation of the text from Mencius. We have three things, the spirits (*shen* 神), the *qi* (氣) and the body form (*xing* 形), in their proper relationship:

'The body is the dwelling place for life (*xing zhe sheng zhi she ye* 形 者 生 之 舍 也).
The *qi* is the plentiful strength of life (*qi zhe sheng zhi chong ye* 氣 者 生 之 充 也).
The spirits are the guide for life (*shen zhe sheng zhi zhi ye* 神 者 生 之 制 也).'

She (舍) is a dwelling place. *Chong* (充) is something which is abundant and strong, a fullness of power. *Zhi* (制) is a control. What are here called the spirits is the same as the will in Mencius. If one of these three loses its place all three will suffer. The text continues:

'If the body loses its place of rest it will deteriorate and wither. If the *qi* is used against that which gives it its real full strength, it will collapse. If the spirits are overactive they become confused.'

Following this the example of a madman is given. The madman cannot avoid falling into fire or water and acting as if he were drunk. The text asks if this is because he lacks a body or spirit or *qi* or will. The answer is no, it is just because he uses those things in a crazy, erratic way.

These kinds of texts help us to put *qi* in its proper context. It is difficult because *qi* is both everything and the specific all at the same time. It is the power of life, but human beings always have a need for guidance. If we need guidance as human beings this guidance has to be in the form of a natural guidance: heaven, spirits, or the Way. I would just remind you, without much commentary, of Laozi chapter 42:

'The *dao* gives birth to one. One gives birth to two. Two gives birth to three. Three gives birth to the ten thousand beings. They carry the *yin* on their back and hold the *yang* in their embrace.'

After that there is the sentence:

'The powerfully blending *qi* are for making harmony (*chong qi yi wei he* 沖 氣 以 為 和).'

Chong (沖) is a kind of rushing or dashing, but at the same time it means to infuse. *Chong qi* is the power of *qi* that comes from the blending of *yin yang* and the collaboration of all the *qi*. The *qi* being *yin* and *yang* are composed in a perfect harmony, so *chong* here implies that there is a blending but of a tranquil nature. It is the power coming from the blending and the harmony which will make life. If you are alive it is because your *qi* are able to maintain a proper harmony, and it is the same thing in nature itself.

XUNZI AND CONSCIOUSNESS

Xunzi was one of the great Confucian philosophers. This is a quotation from chapter 9:

> 'Water and fire possess *qi,* but they do not have life (*sheng* 生). Plants and trees possess life but do not possess awareness (*zhi* 知). Birds and beasts possess awareness but do not possess the sense of duty (i.e. the sense of what is right and appropriate). Human beings possess *qi,* life and awareness, and add to them the sense of duty (*yi* 義).'

Everything has *qi*. Water and fire, which are halfway between what has form and what does not, have *qi,* but it is difficult to say they are living beings because they do not really have a shape. Vegetation not only has *qi* but appears and disappears, so is said to have life. Animals move freely and not only have *qi* and life, but also a kind of consciousness or awareness. This idea is also discussed in chapter 19 of Xunzi in the context of blood and *qi*.

> 'Among all the living beings between heaven and earth, those having blood and *qi* possess awareness (*zhi* 知).'

In the case of some large birds and animals, if one loses its mate or is separated from its group, then even after months or a whole season have passed it is sure to circle its old home when it passes by. This is one kind of awareness, and it is the same character, *zhi* (知) which we translate as knowledge. But this is not enough, and as a human being we have an additional sense of what is appropriate and just.

Qi is therefore everywhere, right from the very beginning, before living beings even appeared. Without *qi* nothing is possible. We will see that again in Zhuangzi chapter 2.

The same idea is presented in the Book of Rites, the Liji, one of the five classics. It is from a treatise on music called the Yueji (樂 記).

> 'By nature man possesses blood and qi, and a heart that allows awareness. Grief as well as joy, elation or anger do not exist permanently within. They are reactions to the incitement of objects. It

is then that the art of the heart intervenes.'

The definition of human beings is that they are made with '*xue qi xin zhi* (血 氣 心 知)'. It means that the proper nature of a human being is to have blood and *qi,* and an awareness coming from or directed by the heart/mind. All the feelings of grief and joy, elation and anger are reactions to external things. But reacting to external things puts the emotions into motion, and they are really a disturbance in the regulation of the *qi* which in turn causes a disturbance to the heart. This is the reason why we have to act according to form and cultivate the art of the heart.

ZHUANGZI AND THE EXPRESSION OF LIFE

Zhuangzi chapter 22 says:

'Man's life is a coming together of *qi* (*qi zhi ju* 氣 之 聚). If it comes together, there is life (*sheng* 生). If it scatters (*san* 散), there is death (*si* 死).'

This sentence is often quoted to explain that life is a process of the condensation of *qi,* to make essences and *qi.* Death is a dispersion of *qi.* The beginning of chapter 2 of Zhuangzi says:

'The great clod belches out *qi* and its name is wind. As long as it does not come forth nothing happens. But when it does then ten thousand hollows begin crying wildly. Can you not hear them, long and drawn out? In the mountain forests that lash and sway there are huge trees a hundred spans around with hollows and openings like noses and mouths, like ears, like jugs, like cups, like mortars, like rifts, like ruts. They roar like waves, whistle like arrows, screech, gasp, cry, wail, moan and howl. Those in the lead cry out *yeee*! Those behind call out *yuuu*! In a gentle breeze they answer faintly, but in a full gale the chorus is gigantic. Then when the fierce wind has passed on all the hollows are empty again. Have you never seen the tossing and trembling that goes on?' (Translated by Burton Watson)

This is the beginning of the text in Chinese:

'*Da kuai yi qi, qi ming wei feng*
大 塊 噫 氣, 其 名 為 風
wu zuo zuo ze wan qiao nu hao
無 作 作 則 萬 竅 怒 呺.'

The great clod stands here for the earth and is the condensation of *yin qi* in a couple relationship with heaven. The clod belches out (*yi* 噫) *qi* and its name, *ming* (名), is wind, *feng* (風). To 'not come forth', *wu zuo* (無 作) is to be without. *Zuo* (作) is to come forth or to start to act. When the wind begins to move then the ten thousand openings start crying wildly, or burst out howling. Wildly (*nu* 怒) is the character for anger, it is an impetuous impulse towards something, a wildness, or a bursting out in anger. To cry (*hao* 號) is to utter some kind of loud sound. Howling is a good word.

A.C. Graham translates these opening sentences as:

'The hugest of clump of soil blows out breath, by name the wind. Better if it were never to start up. For whenever it does ten thousand hollow places burst out howling.'

This is a vision of the earth as a great mass pierced with many hollows, openings or apertures. They are like the caverns, caves, or grottos we see in mountains or among rocks. These openings go deep inside the earth. *Qiao* (竅), hollow, is the character translated as orifice in the medical texts. The upper part of the character *xue* (穴) is also found as part of an ancient expression, *feng xue* (風 穴), the caverns of the wind. These are all the openings by which the wind, coming from heaven, enters into the depths of the earth to stimulate the vital transformations. This is an ancient notion and certainly one of the first models for the body image, because the body itself is a mass, a kind of great clod, but open to penetration by *qi* coming from the outside. So it is not by chance that the character *xue* (穴) is used in Chinese for acupuncture points. This text from Zhuangzi presents an image of the earth, but many of the characters could also be used to describe the human body.

The wind is coming down to earth like clouds belching out *qi,* and the *qi* coming from earth is a reaction to what was sent from heaven. There is always this kind of response. The wind acts first, but there is an aspect of the wind that would be 'better if it were never to start up'. When the wind is motionless it is in nothingness (*wu* 無), having nothing, not even its own blowing. This is a good expression of *qi* before coming into form. When the wind blows we know what kind of wind is blowing and we can see and hear all the expirations and effects of the wind passing through the different beings, as through their effect in the form we can see the various qualities of the *qi.* The example given later in this text is of wind blowing through big trees, and through eight openings making eight kinds of noises. The number eight is of course the traditional number of the winds, representing all the variety of *qi.*

When we perceive something about the wind, we perceive something about *qi.* When *qi* is acting within a form, it is manifesting through something which is perceptible. But is this the only possibility? The Daoists knew that it was not. They understood that there is a way to exist which is without a form, and which is just a merging with the *dao* or uniting with the infinite and undifferentiated potentiality.

In this text we have the concept of *qi* related to the wind when the wind is not acting. If the wind is not blowing we cannot say there is no wind or that the wind does not exist. Zhuangzi is saying something very difficult in these two sentences. We saw earlier the idea of the *qi* being expressed in all living beings and forms, and also being behind everything. We can see this here too. We are beings with *qi* coming forth or blowing, but we know that what we are relies on what has nothing (*wu* 無). *Qi* also exists at the level of the *wu*. This is the root of all the questions of to *qi* which we find in later texts. It is not a double aspect of *qi*; it is the same *qi*, but condensing and appearing through forms, or being imperceptible and existing as a potentiality. This is the reason why this passage is so important and so difficult to understand.

Question: Where does Graham's 'better' come from? ('Better if it were never to start up.')

Graham chose to say 'better', and perhaps he is right, because from the Daoist point of view of Zhuangzi, it is better to come back constantly to the root which is on the side of the *wu* (無), the no-thing, the oneness, the *dao* and so on.

Following this passage in Zhuangzi there is the image of a human being as a big tree with the wind gently prompting a reaction. Then the wind comes wildly and the reaction is wild. We receive qi and we react appropriately according to the qi. But the point is that for the tree, when the fierce wind has passed there is no longer any activity and the hollows are all empty again. They recover their emptiness, and no activity or wind or emotion or anything is retained. This is the problem with us human beings, because even when the wind has passed through us we continue to be full of qi and full of emotions and concerns. We are unable to return to the emptiness that is the free and gentle circulation of qi, and which is the state of the master as presented at the beginning of chapter 2:

'Ziqi of the south wall sat leaning on his armrest staring up at the sky and breathing-vacant and far away as though he'd lost his companion. Yan Chen Ziyou who was standing by his side in attendance said "What is this? Can you really make the body like a withered tree and the mind (xin 心) like dead ashes? The man leaning on the armrest now is not the one who leaned on it before." Ziqi said "You do well to ask the question Yan. Now I have lost myself. Do you understand that?"' (Translation by Burton Watson)

Ziqi had returned to emptiness, and his disciple was astonished. The master was exactly like a dead tree, with everything totally still. We have come back to the same point, and here there is the idea of cultivating the emptiness of the heart in order to cultivate good movement and control of the *qi*.

Another text from Zhuangzi chapter 18 is about the death of his wife:

'Zhuangzi's wife died. When Huizi went to convey his condolences, he found Zhuangzi sitting with his legs sprawled out, pounding on a tub and singing. "You lived with her, she bought up your children and grew old" said Hui, "it should be enough simply not to weep at her death, but pounding on a tub and singing - this is going too far isn't it?"

Zhuangzi said: "You are wrong. When she first died do you think I didn't grieve like anyone else? But I looked back to her beginning and the time before she was born (*wu sheng* 無 生). Not only the time before she was born but the time before she had a body (*wu xing* 無 形). Not only the time before she had a body but the time before she had a spirit (*wu qi* 無 氣). In the midst of the jumble of wonder and mystery a change (*bian* 變) took place and she had a spirit (*you qi* 有 氣). Another change and she had a body. Another change and she was born. Now there has been another change and she is dead. Just like a progression of the four seasons, spring, summer, fall, winter. Now she's going to lie down peacefully in a vast room. If I were to follow after her bawling and sobbing, it would show that I did not understand anything about fate. So I stopped."' (From the translation by Burton Watson.)

The text speaks of the time before she was born. In Chinese, *shi er ben wu sheng* (始 而 本 無 生). *Shi er* (始 而) is in the beginning, and *ben* (本) means both basically and originally. So originally there was a state without life. Moreover, it was without a form (*wu xing* 無 形). There was something even more fundamental, which was to be without *qi* (*wu qi* 無 氣). So this state of being without *qi*, or perceptible *qi*, was a state of complete indistinction. But in the midst of all this indistinctive, wondrous and mysterious state, there is a change. This change, *bian* (變), is another kind of what we will later call original *qi*. In the midst of indistinctness and confusion there is a change and a starting of the process of life. As we saw in Huainanzi 3 [page 41]. Because of this change there is *qi*. Having *qi* and through a change in that *qi* there is form, and having a form and another change there is life or a living being, *sheng* (生). Death is just another change, and so it goes around the circle. The problem here in the Burton Watson translation is that *qi* is translated as spirit which is not really what it is.

Here, then, we have the beginning of the idea of original *qi*. It is not yet called original *qi*, but through these texts we can understand what original *qi* will be. Later on in the medical texts it will be clearly stated that it is the beginning of a process, or the potential of a beginning, towards the manifestation of something. The appearance of the *qi* is also the appearance of *yin yang*.

QI IN MEDICAL TEXTS

We have looked at philosophical texts on *qi* which show the evolution of Chinese thinking before the second century BC. Now we will focus on medical texts, the most basic of which are the Suwen, Lingshu and Nanjing. We will examine these texts in the light of what we have already seen in order to understand how the *qi* which is basic to the theory and practice of medicine is exactly the same as the *qi* which we have already studied in classical texts. What is specific to medical theory is the way in which the *qi* acts according to the movement of life in a human body and how that determines health and disease.

The differentiation of qi

As soon as *qi* is perceptible it manifests as *yin yang qi* with all its expanding and contracting movements and differentiations, and expresses itself through what we can call substance. This is a form, or appearance. When we speak of *qi* in general or of *qi* being everything, we cannot perceive it because it is just a kind of potential. But when some of that potential is realised then there is form, and we can see what kind of *qi* is acting by the transformation enacted through the form. That is the basis of medical theory. By observing *qi* through the forms it takes, by knowing what kind of *qi* is at work, whether all the necessary transformations are proceeding well at each level of the physiology and even the psychology, and by reading signs shown by the form or body, we can know what kind of *qi* is disturbed.

The *qi* acting in the universe serves as a model for the *qi* acting in a human life. Through it we have the complete expression of *yin yang qi*, for example through nutrition/maintenance (*ying* 營) and defence (*wei* 衛), the couple of blood and *qi*, or through the body form. The *qi* of the five elements (*wu xing* 五 行) contain all the possible activities of *qi* at work in the universe and in the human body. Inside a human being this is represented by the *qi* of the five *zang* (臟), with the five *zang* corresponding to the five elements or phases. These five inner movements of life or *qi*, expressed through temperament, tendencies, will and so on, represent all the physiology and psychology of the individual. As we saw in the text from the 25th year of Duke Zhao in the Chunqiu Zuozhuan, the six *qi* of heaven penetrate the earth, eventually provoking disease. Within a human being these six *qi* are also the six great tendencies of the heart/mind, the six emotions or passions:

'In mankind the likes and dislikes, elation and anger (*xi nu* 喜 怒), sorrow and joy (*ai le* 哀 樂), are generated from the six *qi*.'

We saw previously the shift which took place in the value of the associated numbers, and what appeared in the most ancient texts as the six *qi* became, through the prevailing influence of five element theory, the five *qi*. They are nearly the same thing, and we can see in medical texts that six *qi* or six perverse influences are still referred to, but we may also have the five *qi* coming from the surrounding environment and as pathogenic agents. So do not be surprised to sometimes find six *qi* and sometimes five, it is simply that through time five element theory became prevalent and was used as the foundation for all organization of knowledge.

External *qi* pervading everything remained in medical theory as that which made life, but also as that which endangered life. We saw exactly this same understanding expressed earlier in many of the classical texts. Perverse energy is an expression which occurs in texts predating the medical texts. It is an expression that we find from the middle of the third century to the end of the first century BC. Perverse *qi* is *qi* which disturbs the correct functioning of human behaviour or the human mind. It is the cause of physical disease, and medicine understood it as pervading influences able to disturb the correct order of life and *qi*.

In the historical progression of the texts, we see the individual becoming more and more responsible for their own *qi*, with an emphasis on the importance of the centre and the heart/mind. Each time something goes wrong within an individual, it is because they allowed a disorder to settle within them, even if the cause is a perverse influence coming from outside. The individual's own weakness and lack of consciousness and care allowed the perverse *qi* (*xie qi* 邪 氣) to penetrate them, because they were not perfectly harmonised with the flux of life. Human beings are not just the potential of life, they must behave as the expression of this potential of *qi,* then they will always be in a state of natural life and there can be no disease.

Of course nowadays there are very few people who are able to live in this state of being. We have to deal with so many different situations, with the *qi* of our surroundings, with the movement of *qi* by our temperament and emotions, and also with the renewal of *qi* from respiration and food. There is an important link between *qi* and the stomach, and between *qi* and the lung. Nutrition and respiration are both essential for the renewal of *qi*, not only for strength, but also for the quality of the *qi* that creates our life - making character as well as physical strength. Chinese medicine is simply a precise and specific expression of the general understanding of *qi*.

Another point developed in the medical texts is that all *qi* expressed through the five *zang* or through *yin yang,*, is just one *qi* existing in a unity. This oneness is expressed as ancestral *qi* (*zong qi* 宗 氣) or authentic *qi* (*zhen qi* 真 氣) or correct *qi* (*zheng qi* 正 氣). Correct *qi* is not defence or nutrition, or blood and *qi*, or lung *qi*. It is all of these working together with a mutual understanding. The other idea which is not so well developed in medical texts, is that of original *qi* (*yuan qi* 元 氣). Original *qi* is the beginning of a specific life, the potential which has found a way to express itself through an individual bodily form. This is a person's proper nature, the model for the correct functioning and renewal of all the *qi* which makes the movement of their life, and which transforms and keeps the body's form.

QI AND SHEN

Since the human being is responsible for the movement of their own *qi* there is a relationship established between the *qi* and the spirits (*shen* 神). We will not look deeply at this subject, but everything which is said about the *qi* and the movement of *qi* also has to be considered in relation to the spirits. The spirits are not the same thing as the will. We can say 'I am responsible, I decide how I behave, how I eat and breathe', as if it is my will which is responsible for the movement of my *qi* and therefore my good health. In a way this is true, but the point is that this is not the real basis of life, and hence from the Chinese point of view you cannot do something by your own will and judgment, or even knowledge, and be completely right. It is not possible because we are limited in time and space, and in our knowledge and perception of things.

The point is that we have to allow the movement of life within us to be what it is. For the Daoists it leads to the end of seeking and thinking, which means that it is just by letting go and abandoning the idea that it is what I think, know and want which decide who I am. In the fluidity of all life, my own individual life is just an expression of my origin. The ability to be one with the movement of life is the ultimate goal. This is where the *qi* and the spirits are one in the unity. It is at the level of the multiplicity, of the duality of life and the expression of my own particular life and the work I have to do, that we can say the spirits are the guide of the *qi*.

SUWEN CHAPTER 3

Suwen chapter 3 presents the *yin* and the *yang* aspects of *qi*, with the *yang qi* being expressed as the defensive *qi* (*wei qi* 衛氣) and the *yin qi* being expressed through food and nutriment and all the rebuilding and reconstructive power of the essences (*ying qi* 營氣). The *yin yang qi* inside the body expresses the differences between *yin* and *yang*. The *yang* is like the sun, which spreads out but gives a firmness and strength. The *yin* is what is condensed making substance and form, a richness enabling and nourishing the spreading out of the *yang*.

'From ancient times, communication with heaven, the trunk of life, has been rooted in *yin yang*.'

Here we have something which is in the chapter's title, *Sheng qi tong tian* (生 氣 通 天), the *qi* of life communicates with heaven, or the *qi* which gives life is the *qi* of all living beings. The meaning is that the *qi* which makes your life only does so because it is an expression of the natural order of life. This communication with the natural order of life and with heaven above, must be continuously maintained.

The character used for 'trunk' is *ben* (本), which depicts a tree with its roots penetrating the depths. This character is used for trunk, root, and as we have seen, for basis and source. Communication with heaven is what gives the *qi* the ability to make a living being. So if this communication is interrupted or damaged, it is exactly the same thing as damage which is inflicted at the very basis of something. We may try and do whatever we want want with *qi*, but if you are not following heaven or the natural order of life within you in some way, you will not succeed in maintaining either your life or your health.

Whenever there is life, or the expression of something which appears at the moment of birth and disappears at the moment of death, *yin yang* is at work. We need form, and even in the very first stage of development of an embryo, there must be the expression of the power of the *qi* through this form. The form is the first expression of heaven or the natural order, the making of a beginning. With this beginning and with the original *qi* (*yuan qi* 原 氣), it has the potential to realize itself little by little through the growth and development of a form. So each living being and each specific manifestation of life is *yin yang*. After that the whole life can develop.

'In the space between heaven and earth, inside the six junctions (*liu he* 六 合), the *qi* of living beings, in nine territories and through nine orifices (*jiu qiao* 九 竅), in five organs (*zang* 臟), and through twelve rhythms (*jie* 節), all communicates with the *qi* of heaven.'

The six junctions (*liu he* 六 合) are all the *qi* of the universe which exists between heaven and earth, and all the communication between the six qualities of the *qi* of heaven and earth. Every living being exists between heaven and earth and within these exchanges of *qi* which make up the universe as we know it.

The nine territories were the traditional division of Chinese territories into nine provinces, but they are also a division of the body, three by three. There is the division by three in the triple heater, but also the division by nine, for example the nine pulses. Within the body there are differences in the *qi* animating the various areas and functions, and we can feel that in the nine pulses. Also, the term 'nine orifices' is used here for all the communication between the centre and the periphery, upward and downward.

The five *zang* are the inner life and the means by which essences are kept deeply and actively inside. They are five ways to store, manage and regulate life. There are twelve rhythms which represent the twelve meridians. These are twelve ways to articulate the *qi* of life, for example through blood and *qi*. The *qi* which constantly makes life communicates with the *qi* of heaven, and is always in a process of interaction with what gives the natural order of life, our proper nature.

A little further on in chapter 3 it says:

'The *yang qi* is like the sun in heaven. When it loses its place, life is broken and the beings no longer shine. Whether the heavenly influx is regularly distributed depends on the solar radiance. Thus the *yang* soars upwards and ensures defense at the exterior.'

This alludes to the defensive *qi* (*wei qi* 衛 氣), which is like the sun in heaven with the same movement of rising at dawn, extending itself at the surface of the body, and disappearing into the depths at sunset. The movement of defensive *qi* is based exactly on the model of the sun with all the power and capacity of the sun to give warmth and to embrace and stimulate emotions and activity. 'Defence at the exterior' alludes to the best expression of the *yang* movement of *qi* which has a propensity to move outwards.

SUWEN CHAPTER 5

Chapter 5 of the Suwen is one of the most important texts for the theory of medicine, and also for the complete understanding of life through *yin yang* and the five elements. This chapter presents a statement of the most basic theory which has already been at work for 2,000 years.

> 'Cold (*han* 寒), at the utmost (*ji* 極), gives rise (*sheng* 生) to heat (*re* 熱). Heat, at the utmost, gives rise to cold.'

Cold and heat are used here to represent *yin* and *yang* and their manifestations. In life, *yin* and *yang* are the double expression of *qi*, never two *qi*. We must never see *yin* and *yang* as two separate *qi*. With the *yang* movement of *qi* there is evaporation, rising up, expansion and heat, while with the *yin* movement there is condensation, freezing, downward movement and cold. This is a double expression, and the effect of the cold and hot *qi* are felt inside the body. In the process of life, the cold or the *yin* cannot go so far that the return to the *yang* is not possible, because that would be death. So when in disease the cold is severe, the body will warm up, and conversely, if the patient does not die from a high fever, the body will cool down. In physiology, this is also the rule for all ascending and descending, concentrating and expanding movements. It is the same in nature when the warmth comes after the greatest frost of the winter. This is the movement of *qi.*

'Cold *qi* generates (*sheng* 生) unclear (*zhuo* 濁); hot *qi* generates clear (*qing* 清).'

Here we have to understand that unclear and clear are used only for the *yin* and *yang* movements of *qi.* What is unclear is lead by the *yin* and what is clear is lead by the *yang*. We saw this in Huainanzi chapter 3. After this there is a specific reference to particular areas of the body and the digestive process:

'Descending, the clear *qi* (*qing qi* 清 氣) produces (*sheng* 生) diarrhoea with undigested food. Ascending, the unclear *qi* (*zhuo qi* 濁 氣) produces (*sheng* 生) distension and swelling.'

In this case the clear *qi* corresponds to the essences which are assimilated and circulate through the body. This is a *yang* movement. The unclear *qi* corresponds to what is heavy, moves downwards and is finally eliminated. The text refers to that which is not assimilated by the body, but this is only in the context of the digestion of food. If you take the example of body fluids, the thick *ye* (液) are called unclear and the thin *jin* (津) are called clear. But the *ye* fluids are the richest in essences. This seems a contradiction but the *ye* fluids have a *yin* movement. They are more concentrated and do not move quickly as do the *jin* fluids through the layers of the skin or the bulk of the flesh. Instead, they concentrate themselves in the orifices and membranes, which is more of a *yin* movement. It is the opposite for the *jin* fluids which are moved outwards. This is the reason why the *ye* are called unclear.

When we say cold *qi* generates unclear and hot *qi* generates clear, this is the basis of understanding the action of the *yin yang qi* inside the body. In certain circumstances you could say that heat also generates the unclear, for instance when dense body fluids are overheated they become unclear. But this is another level of understanding. We are not speaking here of pathological heat or cold, we are speaking of the normal healthy movements of cold or hot *qi*. Pathology is when this basic movement is disturbed.

'These contrary activities of *yin yang* are diseases, an opposition to the natural movement of life (*ni cong* 逆 從).'

This is one of the most basic definitions of disease and pathology. If the clear *qi* produces diarrhea, it is because warm *qi* is not hot enough, and digestion cannot function properly. Because of this lack of transformation, essences will leave the body via the lower orifices. Not enough heat is coming from the lower heater to support the *yang* of the spleen, so there will be diarrhea with undigested food. The clear is below. Alternatively if there is too much cold then this leads to a distension and swelling throughout the stomach or chest, the congestion rising up through the body.

These are just two examples of *yin* and *yang qi* losing their place, not being in good balance and not cooperating with one another. Cold and heat have to be in harmony in such a way that all the heat rises up from the *yang* of the kidneys, the authentic *yang*, leading to the correct functioning of everything and allowing the clear to be under the *yang* movement of distribution. The cold also has to be in the right place and in the right proportion, retaining, but not blocking or injuring the heat. So the activity of the *qi* is primarily seen as *yin yang* and with the first disturbance of cold and heat comes the natural opposition to the correct movement of life. This what is called disease. Each time there is a movement which is not the natural movement of *qi*, it is said to be disease. This is interesting because this definition of disease very different to that of western medicine. Disease for the Chinese is that there is something wrong in the balance of *qi*.

After that we have an example of the clear and the unclear:

> 'Thus, clear *yang* makes (*wei* 為) heaven and unclear *yin* makes earth. Ascending, the earth *qi* makes clouds, descending the heaven *qi* makes rain. Rain (*yu* 雨) comes from earth *qi* and clouds (*yun* 雲) come from heaven *qi*.'

Here we can see the production of the universe via the double movement of *yin yang qi*, and the model in nature for all the processing of liquids that goes on inside the human body. The images of water, clouds and rain are used because this is the best way to understand *qi* since water also has a changing form. It can be water, vapour or ice. Water is universally considered to be the best example of the way *qi* works. Here the *yin yang qi* is acting between heaven and earth under the attraction of heaven and the receptivity of earth. The clear *yang*, the ascending vapour, makes clouds, and the unclear *yin*, descending, makes rain which penetrates the earth with a movement of condensation. So there is always an exchange, and the constitution and reconstitution of what is heaven and earth inside the human body is maintained. For example, it is the ascending of the clear *yang* which enables us to renew the 'heavenly *qi*' in our head, allowing the correct functioning of the brain, the sense organs and the heart. A great deal of pathology arises when the clear *yang* cannot ascend. It is through this movement that the physiology and psychology of everything pertaining to heaven exists within us.

With this kind of text we cannot interpret just at one level, we must take in the whole picture. With the rain coming from earth *qi* the clouds evaporate through the attraction of heaven. The rain which falls from heaven also falls because of the attraction of earth. Within the body there is a similar attraction upwards and downwards. For instance, the kidneys are the basis and foundation, but they are also able to attract things into the depths, and to give life to the power of the *yang*. If we consider the lung, the lung attracts the *qi* in order to spread it around the whole body. But it also exerts a pressure downwards to make rain or the good circulation of fluids. At each level of our life and functioning we have something similar to this great movement of *yin yang qi* in nature. After this the text continues:

'So the clear *yang* appears (*chu* 出) at the upper orifices (*shang qiao* 上 竅), and the unclear *yin* appears at the lower orifices (*xia qiao* 下 竅).'

Here we have the couple of ascending and descending, the *yang* movement pushing the essences and the clear *yang* upwards to the head and the sense organs, and the unclear *yin* going to the lower orifices, and in the process of digestion becoming what is eliminated.

'The clear *yang* spreads up (*fa* 發) to the texture of the skin (*cou li* 腠 理), and the unclear *yin* goes (*zou* 走) to the five *zang*. The clear *yang* gives fullness (*shi* 實) to the four limbs, and the unclear *yin* returns (*gui* 歸)to the six *fu*.'

This seems to be a contradiction. Here the unclear *yin* goes to the five *zang*, in which case it cannot be the waste which is eliminated. We have to take 'clear' and 'unclear' as the double movement of *qi* in all things. So what is *yang qi* goes outwards, diffusing through the skin, and permeating the four limbs for muscular movement. It is a centrifugal movement, while the *yin* has a centripetal movement with the essences going inwards to the five *zang* and six *fu*. In this double activity of *yin* and *yang,* the *yang* makes the strength and the *yin* makes the substances.

'Water is (*wei* 為) *yin* and fire is *yang. Yang* makes (*wei* 為) the *qi* and *yin* makes the tastes (*wei* 味). The tastes return (belong to, *gui* 歸) to the (body) form (*xing* 形), the form returns to the *qi*. the *qi* return to the essences (*jing* 精), the essences return to the transformations (*hua* 化).'

We have here another couple within *yin yang*, *qi* and taste. The tastes are all the substances able to renew the essences and life. After that there is a sentence which says that the tastes return to the body form, the form returns to the *qi*, the *qi* return to the essences and the essences to the transformations. All of these statements are linked by the character *gui* (歸), to return, or to belong to, to go back to one's place of origin. *Gui* conveys the idea of an arrival somewhere by someone carrying a duster and a dustpan. This represents the wife or bride. It is literally the arrival of the bride at the house of her husband, which is not exactly a return since she has never been there before. What is important is the sense of going to a place where you are able to fulfil your proper nature, and completely realise who you are. Therefore the tastes are for the body form, they are to maintain the essences and to build the form of the body. But the form itself is the place for the expression of the *qi*. Without form there is no manifested *qi*. The *qi* keep the essences inside and make and sustain life. They make life through transformations. Throughout this passage then, the prevalent notion is that of *qi*.

'The essences eat (or feed on) (*shi* 食) the *qi*. The body form eats (or feeds on) the tastes (*wei*

味). Transformations produce (*sheng* 生) the essences.'

The essences feed the five *zang* and enable them to release the *qi* which makes our physiology and psychology. It is through the transformations of digestion that we can keep and assimilate the essences. But it is also through the perpetual transformations which are made by the *qi* that we may keep the body fluids in the right place and the essences acting normally.

'The *qi* produce the body form (*xing* 形). The tastes injure (*shang* 傷) the body form. The *qi* injure the essences. The essences, through transformations, make (*wei* 為) *qi*. The *qi* are injured by the tastes.'

There are many practical examples of this. What is interesting is to see that the relationship between *qi* and essences is a very strong one. In fact there is a triple relationship between *qi* and essences. There is the relationship of the *qi* with transformations through the essences, but the *qi* are also in relationship with the body form and with the tastes. *Qi* is at the centre of everything which is made by the five aspects of the maintenance of life: the *qi,* the essences, the body form, the tastes and the transformations.

Qi and fire

We will now look at the relationship of fire with *qi*. Both *qi* and fire are aspects of *yang*:

'Strong fire (*zhuang huo* 壯 火) feeds on (*shi* 食) *qi* and the *qi* are nourished (*shi* 食) by gentle fire. Strong fire dispels (*san* 散) the *qi* and gentle fire produces (*sheng* 生) *qi*.'

The relationship between *qi* and essences is the basic *yin yang* relationship of the body and of everything which makes the movement, transformation, warming, rhythm, and strength necessary to keep the essences inside and in such a way that they can be active. But we can also speak of tastes and *qi* and therefore have a dialectic between the *qi* and the body form. The relationship between the body form and the *qi* is between that which has a form to express life and that which operates life inside that form. An analogous relationship exists between the essences or the *qi* and the tastes.

So this 'gentle fire' (*shao huo* 少 火) describes the qi when it is transforming well and maintaining balance with the *yin*. It is able to do this because it is sustained by the moderate power of the *yang*, by the original fire or the fire of *ming men*, which is always a gentle fire giving good rhythm to the circulation and allowing all the operations of life to be performed well, without destroying essences, body form or tastes. If the fire is too strong, then that will destroy the essences, and if they are destroyed they cannot feed or make *qi.*

Heat and cold

Other relationships between the *qi* and the body form are spoken of later in the text of Suwen chapter 5:

'Cold injures (*shang* 傷) the body form (*xing* 形) and heat injures the *qi.* Injury to the *qi* gives pain (*tong* 痛), Injury to the body form gives swelling (*zhong* 腫). Thus if there is first pain and then swelling, the *qi* injures the body form, and if there is first swelling and then pain, the body form injures the *qi.*'

Cold is a *yin* movement of *qi* and so it will go to what is a *yin* manifestation in the body form, but heat is on the *yang* side and will have a direct relationship with the *qi* as representative of the *yang.* The *yin* can therefore injure the *qi,* and give the *yang* power of the *qi* a destroying strength, while cold can stop the transformations effected by the *qi,* and can stop the transformation and maintenance of the body form. When there is injury to the body due to cold and the *yin* movement of *qi*, there is a kind of condensation which gives rise to swelling. The *qi* no longer transforms and transports the body fluids and there will be oedema. When the *qi* is injured first, for example by heat, initially there will be pain and afterwards swelling. What is clear is that the *qi* always precedes the form. There is no form if there is no *qi*. There is no maintenance or transformation of the form without *qi*. On the other hand, without a form there can be no expression of *qi*.

The five atmospheric influences and the five emotions

The text goes on to present wind, heat, dryness, cold and dampness, which are the five *qi* of the environment, and expressions of the *qi* of nature. They are also pathogenic agents within the human body. The five *qi* generated inside the human body by the five *zang* are manifest through the five emotions.

> 'Heaven has four seasons (*si shi* 四 時) and five elements (*wu xing* 五 行) for generating (*sheng* 生), growing (*zhang* 長), gathering (*shou* 收) and burying (*cang* 藏), to produce cold, heat, dryness, dampness and wind.'

These are the four natural actions of each of the four seasons: generating for the spring, growing for the summer, gathering for the autumn and burying, or keeping in the depths, for the winter. Cold, heat, dryness, dampness and wind are the five atmospheric influences representing all the *qi* of nature.

> 'A human has five *zang* and, by transformations (*hua* 化), five *qi*, to produce elation (*xi* 喜), anger (*nu* 怒), sadness (*bei* 悲), grief (*you* 憂) and fear (*kong* 恐).'

These are not the seven emotions, or the six expressions of the will. They are five because we are within the model of the five elements. Everything which is generated within, not only as the five *qi* but as all the activity and physiology of the activity of the five *zang*, influences the mind and behaviour as these five great tendencies of the temperament.

The text goes on to discuss the *qi* and the body form. The body form is the first thing to be exposed to the *qi* of nature or of the exterior. The point being made is that the emotions can also penetrate the bodily form and disturb the inner balance. Everything which happens in the body is under the authority of one's own *qi*.

Elation and anger injure the *qi*. This is a very old idea which we find in Zhuangzi. *Yin yang qi* is injured by all the emotions that we allow to settle in ourselves. Violent anger injures the *yin* and violent elation injures the *yang*. Due to the consequent weakening the *qi* moves upwards and the vital circulation becomes congested. Vitality therefore leaves the body. This all occurs when things are not well balanced. If elation and anger are not well regulated, if cold and heat are excessive, then life is no longer strong. Life must be regulated to keep it in such a way that what occurs on the exterior will not really disturb the *qi* or the body form.

SUWEN CHAPTER 2

Suwen chapter 2 presents the four seasons, which are not only the model for the *qi* and all its variations in nature, but also the rhythm which all life is subject to. We observe the four seasons from outside, but as living beings among the ten thousand other living beings, we are part of the universe and feel the same rhythm of the four seasons inside ourselves.

'The three months of spring are called springing up and unfolding (*fa chen* 發 陳). Heaven and earth together produce life (*sheng* 生) and the ten thousand beings are invigorated. At night, one goes to bed; at dawn, one gets up. One paces in the courtyard with great strides, hair loose, body at ease, exerting the will (*zhi* 志) for life, letting live, not killing; giving, not taking away; rewarding, not punishing. This corresponds

with the spring *qi* (*chun qi* 春氣). It is the way
(*dao* 道) that maintains the drive of life. To go
against (*ni* 逆) this would injure the liver, causing
disturbance due to cold in summer, through an
insufficient contribution to growth.'

During the spring, if we behave in a spring-like
manner, it is not only because we absorb the quality
of spring from nature and act accordingly, but also
because in our own lives there is a feeling of surging
upwards and springing forth which we have to follow.
This internal spring is felt in the season of spring and
also in the springtime of life, youth. It is found in each
situation which is spring-like and in which we have to
follow this kind of rhythm. When it is spring in nature it
is also spring within my individual life, in my psychology
and physiology. And there will be difficulties if I oppose
this natural movement of spring by behaviour which
goes against the season.

I must accompany the movement of spring in nature
with corresponding movements in my own body, for
instance 'pacing the courtyard with great strides, hair
loose, body at ease', and let the blood run in the muscles
and invigorate the head, freeing the circulation of the
liver and allowing it to flow right up to the extremities.
At the same time I have to exert my will, but only in a
certain way because I must act in accordance with the
moment of time. I must not force myself in this, but do

it just because it fits with how I am at this point in the seasonal cycle.

To go against this vital movement of *qi* would injure the liver. Every time a certain quality of *qi* prevails within my own personal rhythm, if I block it or go against it, it will create a disorder leading to an imbalance, which is disease. The importance of Suwen chapter 2 is in this perspective of the inner life which is really the basis for the unfolding of the *qi*.

LINGSHU CHAPTER 75

Lingshu chapter 75 is interesting because it describes the variety of *qi*.

'Needling regulates (tunes) the *qi* (*tiao qi* 調 氣). *Qi* accumulates in the stomach in order to circulate as nutrition (*ying* 營) and defence (*wei* 衛), each according to its own pathways.'

Tiao qi (調 氣) is a very common phrase. *Tiao* (調) is a character which is often used to express any kind of treatment influencing the *qi*, or a function or meridian. It means to regulate, to tune as with a musical instrument, to blend in the right proportions, or to adjust. It is not really the result which is important here, it is the action. So the definition of acupuncture here is *tiao qi* (調 氣). You do something with the *qi* which is like tuning a piano, and you try to make it more harmonious.

There follows a presentation of *qi* in the human body. The classical texts never give a complete clarification of all the various types of *qi* in the body, but here we have a presentation of several types, the ancestral (*zong* 宗), the authentic (*zhen* 真), the correct (*zheng* 正) and the perverse (*xie* 邪).

'*Qi* accumulates (*ji* 積) in the stomach in order to circulate (*tong* 通) as nutrition and defence, each according to its own pathways.'

This idea is found in a lot of texts. Everything starts with the stomach, especially in the Neijing school. This represents posterior heaven for the renewal of *qi*. We are not speaking here of body fluids or substances or food itself proceeding through the intestines. We are only focusing on the renewal of *qi* by the work of the stomach.

The character *ji* (積) can also be used with a more negative connotation, to mean a blockage. But in many texts *ji* has a positive meaning, and in these cases there is another aspect to it. The accumulation is not a substantial one. It is not a piling up, it is rather that something comes again and again, and gets better and better. For instance, when you accumulate experiences or knowledge you do not pile them up, but you make your vision more accurate and clear. When you repeat the movements of *qi gong* (氣 功) each morning you accumulate something which is a good functioning of your *qi*.

In this text, when *qi* is accumulated by the stomach the meaning is not that the *qi* is piling up in the stomach, but that the *qi* is regularly renewed by the proper functioning of the stomach. The *qi* comes, is renewed and then released. All the *qi* which is accumulated circulates, *tong* (通). So there is no contradiction here between accumulation and circulation. Circulation is made by means of the constructive *ying qi* and defensive *wei qi* each following their own way.

Ancestral qi

'The ancestral *qi* (*zong qi* 宗 氣) flows to the sea, it goes down, flowing to the street of *qi*; upwards it goes to the respiratory pathway.'

The sea referred to here is the sea of *qi* in the middle of the chest. Street of *qi* is the point name of Stomach 30, but it is also the name of all transportation and guidance of the *qi* in the legs.

Authentic qi

The next definition is for authentic *qi* (*zhen qi* 真 氣) which is received from heaven:

'The authentic *qi* is that which is received from heaven. Together with the *qi* from food it gives the person (*shen* 身) their force.'

'That which is received from heaven' we can understand either as respiration or the origin. What is given by heaven is our own original nature, our destiny. But the text continues saying that together with the *qi* coming from food it gives full strength to the individual and their body form. In this case, because the authentic *qi* is specifically related with the *qi* from food, we can understand the authentic *qi* as *qi* of heaven, and the *qi* of heaven as respiration, as opposed to food which is *qi* of earth.

The problem is that the text does not conform with the definitions we use in English now. Here, authentic *qi* is used for the *qi* of respiration, but nevertheless as the *qi* of heaven it is not only respiration but the whole order of life. So we can see that in another context it is possible to understand authentic *qi* not specifically as the *qi* of respiration but as *qi* which follows the natural order of heaven in myself. When all my *qi* follows the natural order it is expressing the full potential of my origin, and it is natural, heavenly and authentic. We have to be clear about the difference between authentic *qi* and between what is called correct *qi* (*zheng qi* 正 氣).

Correct qi

'The correct *qi* (*zheng qi* 正 氣) are the correct winds (*zheng fang* 正 風). They each come from a specific direction or territory. They are neither the wind causing (pathological) fullness, nor the wind causing (pathological) emptiness.'

The correct wind of the north is the wind or *qi* which comes from the north. The north is the same thing as the winter solstice, and the south is the same thing as the summer solstice. The west is the autumn equinox and the east is the spring equinox. The four intermediate directions mark the beginning of each of the four seasons. For example, the north-east is the beginning of spring. It is normal to have a particular wind coming from the north when you are in the depths of winter. This is what is called a correct wind. It would not be correct if you had a winter wind blowing during the beginning of autumn, or a winter wind coming from the east or the west. That would be a perverse wind. So what is called the correct *qi* in this text refers to every kind of *qi* being in the right place at the right time.

If something goes wrong you can rectify it, and *zheng* (正) also means to rectify. So *zheng* is to follow the rule and not to overdo it. Very often not following the rule is the same thing as overdoing something. This is an idea from the Han Dynasty. *Zheng* is made with the character meaning to stop (止). It is the mark of the footprint. You stop when you have reached the limit or line (一). Not to be able to stop is seen as the beginning of all kinds of disorder. It is not good if the north wind extends itself by blowing northeast or northwest, or if the winter wind continues to blow during the spring. That is also a disturbance because it is not following the regular alternation and movement of the *qi* in nature.

We have the image of the eight winds, but also of the five *qi* or the five *zang*. They must all be in the right balance, not prevailing over or dominating the other. It is possible to see every kind of cycle or relationship between the five elements behind that. When nothing is going wrong, when everyone is following their own destiny and doing what they have to do, that is correct *qi*. Then we can understand what comes next in the text which is perverse *qi*, *xie qi* (邪 氣). Perverse *qi* is exactly the opposite of *zheng qi* both inside and outside the body.

Perverse qi

The character *xie* (邪) is a representation a canine

tooth. What is interesting is that this character was also used in place of another with the meaning of a soiled or stained garment, something that is no longer new and pure, but polluted. Consequently the character has taken on the meaning of depraved, something that does not follow the normal rules, is not in the right place and order, and is perverse or evil. The Lingshu is a medical text, so the meaning of *xie* is primarily 'pathogenic' since *xie* is not used as evil in medical texts. But for the Chinese the character certainly has this broader meaning, even though evil may be a little bit too moral in connotation for us as a translation.

The definition given here for *xie qi* (邪 氣) is that it is *xu feng* (虛 風), the wind taking advantage of an emptiness. This wind behaves like a thief, and injures human beings. Here we have the idea of perverse *qi* as *qi* which is out of place. It is either extending too much, or coming at the wrong time and in the wrong place, as for instance untimely cold during the summer. It is interesting that it is called *xu feng* (虛 風). This kind of *qi* always takes advantage of a deficiency in your own system. If you are functioning completely normally and healthily there is no reason for an excess of cold or an unexpected wind to surprise and disturb you. But this kind of wind can harm you, and it behaves like a robber. The image of the robber wind is a popular one. It robs your life because it destabilizes and disorganizes all the *qi* making up your physiology, the process of your transformations, the storing of your essences, and the maintenance of your body form.

Suwen chapter 2 says:

'When the *qi* in heaven is clear and peaceful (*qing jing* 清 淨) then the light is brilliant (*guang ming* 光 明). If heaven's virtue is stored indefinitely, nothing descends. When heaven retains its brilliant virtue (*tian ming* 天 明), then sun and moon are deprived of radiance (*bu ming* 不 明), perverse influences (*xie* 邪) injure all hollows and orifices and thus the *yang qi* is blocked from within and without. The *qi* of earth cannot show its brilliance, clouds and mists no longer produce essences (*jing* 精), and this meeting above does not produce the descending white dew. Exchange and communication do not occur. The ten thousand beings no longer follow their destiny in life, even the great trees perish in large numbers.

'Once the *qi* has become unhealthy (*e qi* 惡 氣) there is no more surging of life (*bu fa* 不 發). Winds and rains are in disorder, the pearly dew does not descend and vegetation no longer prospers. The robber winds rush around in gusts, torrential rains keep pouring down. The four seasons of heaven earth no longer support each other. The way has been lost. Even before being completed everything is already destroyed.

'Only the saints, following the natural course, themselves escape all harm and save the ten thousand beings from extinction. The *qi* of life (*sheng qi* 生 氣) does not run dry.'

This is an important Chinese text because it describes the human body and the cosmos using the same vocabulary and characters. It suggests that we should be clear and peaceful (*qing jing* 清 淨), calm and serene in our heart/mind. This is not the heart as one of the five *zang*, but as the centre of the self, the oneness of the five *zang*. This heart is really heaven. 'Heaven in me is virtue, earth in me is *qi*', as is said in Lingshu chapter 8.

When the clear and pure essences are nourished through the work of the five *zang*, then life is brilliant and the radiance of the spirits, *shen ming* (神 明) is able to appear. This is the radiance, the splendour, the light and the enlightenment coming from the presence of the spirits because of the calmness of the heart and the lightness of heaven. In this case, nothing can happen to you and all works well. But if heaven's virtue is stored indefinitely then nothing descends. Heaven retains its brilliant virtue but the sun and moon are deprived of their radiance. Nothing comes from the heart because there is a kind of blockage. There is no longer any display or spreading out of the influences or inspiration or light coming from the spirits. If the heart cannot spread this influence, the sense organs and upper orifices are deprived of their radiance and cannot function properly. And anywhere in the body the harmful results of this deprivation of inner radiance will be felt.

When this happens and the heart is not spreading the light of life, then perverse influences injure the hollows and orifices. In all the openings of the body, visible and invisible, there is a possibility for robber winds to enter, and the body is vulnerable to all the potential problems of *qi* at the level of *yin* and *yang*. *Yang qi* is blocked and the *qi* of earth cannot show its brilliance. Clouds and mists no longer produce essences, so there is disaster and all kinds of diseases may arise. In such a condition there is no chance of remaining in good health, and little by little it is impossible, through the transformations of the *qi*, to reproduce the essences that are the basis of life. Although the robber winds come from outside, this situation arises because of an emptiness within.

Just after this passage, Suwen chapter 2 continues with a description of a catastrophic situation in which everything is out of order and out of season. There is constant wind and rain and disorder. Nothing follows the correct order of life and the result is disastrous for all living beings. The text says:

'Only the saints, following the natural course,

themselves escape all harm and save the ten thousand beings from extinction. The *qi* of life does not run dry.'

We know that as human beings we will face difficulties, but we must also acknowledge that it is always possible not to give way to the disruption of our *qi*. A sage is always able to maintain the regulation of life, perhaps even when dying. To be human is to follow the natural order, and it is also the only way to nourish life and be healthy. If you are healthy you follow the natural order in yourself, you have light in your heart, and a spiritual life which is also the natural life. So not only is there no harm for the sage but there is also a kind of virtue and influence emanating from him, permeating others and helping them to restore the balance of their lives. This is an idea which is found in Daoism, but which is included in the text here as a different kind of perspective.

If you are really weak, perverse *qi* could be any kind of influence taking advantage of your weakness. If you are not weak it could be unexpected circumstances, irregular atmospheric conditions, or strong pressure in the prevailing *qi*, which becomes perverse because it is so strong that it enters and harms you. But if you keep your heart peaceful, you will be able to maintain all your defences in the correct balance in order to preserve the correct functioning of your *zang* and *zheng qi* (正 氣).

In this way you will not be overwhelmed by influences coming from outside, even if there is a lot of pressure.

ORIGINAL QI

Original *qi (yuan qi* 原 氣) is not really presented or explained in the Neijing. The notion of *yuan qi* (原 氣) in Chinese thought was not elaborated at this time. It developed slowly and came later with characters describing the concept of origin. The best texts are Nanjing difficulties 8 and 66. In Nanjing difficulty 8, within the part of the text dealing with the pulses, there is an unusual passage. It speaks of an instance when there is no imbalance in the pulses but the person dies. The reason given is that the root that sustains the patient's life is finished or cut. The text says:

> 'The twelve meridians (*jing mai* 經 脈) are connected with the source (*yuan* 原) of the vital *qi* (*sheng qi* 生 氣). The source of the vital *qi* is the root and foundation (*gen ben* 根 本) of the twelve meridians, that is the *qi* moving between the kidneys (*shen jian dong qi* 腎 間 動 氣).'

Sheng qi (生 氣) can be translated differently according to the context. It could be life-giving *qi* or the *qi* of life, or the *qi* sustaining living beings, or vital *qi*.

Here the text is talking of the source of this life-giving *qi*, and the character used in the Nanjing is *yuan* (原). Etymologically *yuan* is made with flowing water (泉), which is white, pure and clear. The part surrounding it is the rock or cliff from where this water flows (厂).

There are a lot of ideas contained in this. The water is pure at the origin of the source. It is afterwards that the water may become unclear or turbid with rain or mud, or with all the things people wash in the water. The general idea is that the water keeps running, and by doing so it becomes clear again. The challenge is to be able to accept the dirt of the world, just as we have to accept heat and cold and so on, and just continue flowing onwards towards the sea. Water is a model of life because it always follows its own nature. By doing this it follows a movement, and by keeping to that it is able to remain clear, or become clear once again. It is the same in our own nature. We have a source and an origin that is completely pure and clean. If we speak in terms of *qi*, *yuan qi* is the potential of *qi*, which is then expressed in a specific form. This is our proper nature which we must retain.

Coming back to the quotation from Nanjing difficulty 8, *ben* (本) is a root, a basis or foundation. The character *gen* (根) is also made with the image of a tree (木), but is used more for the physical roots themselves. *Gen* can be used with the more figurative meaning but *ben* has a wider use because it expresses how the tree is planted and rooted, and its use as a metaphor is greater. The title of Lingshu chapter 8 is Benshen (本 神), rooted in spirits. The spirits are what hold the whole life, the basis and the foundation. Sometimes this is translated as natural spirits, since the basis of my life must be what is natural to my life.

The idea of *ming men* (命 門) appears in the Neijing but it is not exactly the same as in the Nanjing. Nanjing difficulties 8 and 66 speak of *yuan* (原) and *yuan qi* (原 氣) while difficulties 36 and 39 speak of *ming men*. They do not appear together, but there is not much difference between them. It is really a question of evolving vocabulary because when the Nanjing was written, a complete synthesis of terminology had not yet been made. The Nanjing was intended to explain the Neijing, but the Neijing we have now is not the same Neijing as they had then.

'The *qi* moving between the kidneys' is a very old conception of the origin. It represents the *yang* between the *yin*, with the movement of the *qi* as *yang* and the two kidneys representing the *yin* or water. This resembles the trigram for water *kan* (坎) which has one *yang* line between two *yin* lines (☵). The origin and its constant presence in the body are represented frequently in the Neijing by the kidneys. If the kidneys are really seen as the mediation between the origin and the development of an individual life, it is related to the idea of water as the first of the five elements, and as the origin of everything.

Another aspect which is perhaps not stated overtly but which is nevertheless understood is the way that we speak of heaven and earth but also of *yin* and *yang*. Heaven comes first and earth second, but in the couple of *yin yang*, *yin* comes first and *yang* second. Heaven is always first because heaven gives the initiative and the beginning to a process, then earth follows, obeys, gives form and achieves completion, but only under the authority of heaven's inspiration. In a living being we have the origin or original impulse, the *yuan qi*, but as soon as we have the expression of something within that, the *yin* must come first. We have to have a form for the *qi* to become specific, and inside the form we always need the *yin* and the essences in order to release the *qi*. As we saw in Suwen chapter 5: 'the essences by transformation make *qi*'. The production of *qi* is always based on the *yin*. It is always by calmness and tranquillity that the movement and quality of *qi* is maintained.

On the *ren mai* (任 脈) there are two seas of *qi* (Ren 6 and Ren 17), the movement of the *yin* allowing the display and renewal of the *yang*. *Ming men* (命 門) fire is the original impulse that sustains all the movement of life just as the original impulse sustains the movement of an arrow until the end of its flight. The original fire or *yang* sustains the functioning of all the organs, and all the *qi* of the organs in the body until the end.

This vision of the origin is not only in the past but also the strength of the present. A river remains a river because of its source. If you cut off the source there is no more river. In the character *yuan* (原) there is always something which is flowing from the source. If our life is comparable with the river there must be something that is continually being given by the origin. The origin is always present and always sustaining life. If we cut off the origin we cut off the source and that is the end of life. In this way we say that the twelve meridians are connected to the source. In other texts it also says that the extraordinary meridians *du mai* (督 脈) and *ren mai* (任 脈) are connected to the origin. They do not use exactly the same vocabulary but the meaning is the same, and it is this character *yuan* (原) which is used, not the other one, (元), which can also be used for original *qi*.

The character *yuan* (元) has something above and descending represented by the top line (一), that which is coming from heaven for instance. The second line represents the goodness descending (兀). This traditional etymological interpretation from the first and second centuries AD does not reflect the historical one that what is above is descending on a man, represented by his two legs. This is the idea of *yuan* as something from heaven descending upon us. It is the origin, but more as the principle of the origin, and the beginning of a very specific process. The difference between these two characters for *yuan* is that the first (元) is a gift from heaven, my true nature, and the principle of my whole life. It states that what is at the origin is natural to me and is the way I ought to be. In the other character (原) there is the suggestion of a continuous emergence of the original pattern, which allows everything to function. So my *qi* will be patterned on the origin and the true natural order, flowing in the right direction and in the right pace, without any kind of perversion.

Coming back to the *qi* moving between the kidneys, we also have *dong qi* (動 氣). *Dong* (動) means to move or movement, but it is also to beat, as in the beating of the heart or the pulse. A *dong mai* (動 脈) is an artery, a circulatory vessel with a beating movement. It is also the beating that defines a living being or those who are able to move. *Dong* suggests the idea of all the movement of life. We cannot see this *qi* but it is for the movement of life, and later it appears through the form the *qi* has made possible. Nanjing difficulty 8 continues:

> 'This *qi* is the foundation of the five *zang* and the six *fu*, the root (*gen* 根) of the twelve meridians, the gate (*men* 門) of exhalation and inhalation. The source (*yuan* 原) of the triple heater. It is also called the guardian of the spirits against perverse influences (*shou xie zhi shen* 守 邪 之 神).'

The image of a gate or door (*men* 門) is very often

linked in classical texts with the root (*ben* 本) of something. It indicates dialectic between what is at the root and what is in the opening.

If the *qi* is the root and foundation of the twelve meridians, of the five *zang* and the six *fu*, of exhalation and inhalation, what else can it be? Being the source of the triple heater is explained in difficulty 66, which presents the idea of original *qi* but with the image of the source. The *qi* is also called the guardian against the perverse influences.

> 'The *qi* moving between the kidneys (*shen jian dong qi* 腎 間 動 氣), below the navel, is the vital destiny of a human being (*ren zhi sheng ming* 人 之 生 命). It is the root and foundation (*gen ben* 根 本) of the twelve meridians. Hence it is called original (*yuan* 原). The triple heater is the envoy able to make differentiation (*bie shi* 別 使) for the original *qi* (*yuan qi* 原 氣). It (the triple heater) masters the circulation of the three *qi* (*san qi* 三 氣) and their passage through the five *zang* and the six *fu*.'

How can we guard the spirits and go against the perverse influences if not by being faithful to the original pattern? To be faithful to that and then follow the natural movement of *qi* just as water follows its own natural course, to be at one with the natural order and heaven, that is the way to guard the spirits. The text continues:

> 'Hence this *qi* constitutes the root and foundation of man (*ren zhi gen ben* 人 之 根 本). Once the root is cut, the stem and leaves wither.'

In the Huainanzi it also says that if you draw a tree by the root it will come with the last of the leaves, but if you try to draw it by one leaf or one branch you just get that leaf or that branch and nothing else.

When Nanjing 66 says: 'The *qi* moving between the kidneys, below the navel, is the vital destiny of a human being (*ren zhi sheng ming* 人 之 生 命)' it is not referring to a specific anatomical location because 'between the kidneys' is not below the navel. But this is not written from an anatomical perspective. This text is considering the *qi* which is the foundation, and which is not exactly located but is represented centrally in the lower abdomen or heater, at the very foundation of the trunk and the whole being. 'Below the navel' is the sea of *qi* (Ren 6) on the *ren mai* (任 脈), and all the other points which allude to the origin of life. It is also where we have the link with the power to reproduce life. All this is mentioned in Nanjing difficulties 36 and 39. *Ming men* (命 門) and the power to reproduce life must be linked with the power to produce life. What gives me life also gives me the power to give life to another being.

All that is related to the kidneys, but not to the physical kidneys in their correct anatomical location, but to this whole area below the navel where they are present with the quality of their *qi*.

The *qi* moving between the kidneys is the vital destiny (*sheng ming* 生 命) of a human being. The character *ming* (命) has here the meaning of destiny. It is what I am supposed to do and be, following the natural order of things. For example, if the king sends a messenger with a mandate to do something, that is *ming*. The messenger has been given a mission to accomplish, and the means to do so. It is the same thing with human destiny. My true nature is my mandate, being what I am. But being my life, it is also my destiny. I fulfil my destiny by just behaving according to the *qi* given to me at my origin.

The reference to the triple heater is specific to the Nanjing. It is here because it is three as the expression of the multiplicity. We have the one: one original *qi* in the likeness of heaven and in my unity and oneness. But we are also living in the multiplicity because the life which is one is also expressed through a bodily form existing between heaven and earth, and with all the diversity of the twelve meridians and so on. This diversity is expressed at the first level by the number three, which is the natural number of *qi*. Through the number three we perceive the manifestation of the oneness of the origin. Two is the pre-requisite of the manifestation, not the manifestation itself. Two is differentiation within the wholeness of one, allowing the inner rhythm of life in the *qi* (*yin* and *yang*, heaven and earth) to appear. *Yin* and *yang* cannot exist or be seen in themselves separately, only in their multiple intertwinings.

Many other texts mention this idea, for example the Daoists talk of the *san yi* (三 一). The meaning of *san yi* is the three represented in the oneness. We can represent the one only with the three. Three is necessary for the expression of *qi* in form, and for life in all its diversity. The three kinds of *qi* are explained in a variety of texts as corresponding to each of the levels of the triple heater, with the *zong qi* (宗 氣) in the upper heater, the constructive *ying qi* (營 氣) in the middle heater and the defensive *wei qi* (衛 氣) in the lower heater. The triple heater is triple for that reason; it is the relationship between the one and the three.

When the text says that the triple heater is the envoy able to make differentiation (*bie shi* 別 使) for the original *qi* (*yuan qi* 原 氣), the differentiation or separation itself, the *bie* (別), leads to the appearance of something. In fact it is only by separation that something can happen and appear. For instance in the Huainanzi and in other texts, which present a possible theory of genesis it is said that in the midst of the chaos and the infinite but undifferentiated potential there is a separation of the clear and unclear in order to make heaven and earth appear. *Bie* is the distinction between appearance and specificity in the functioning of *qi*, but based, and remaining based, on the origin and original impulse. The foundation for the three kinds of *qi (zong, wei* and *ying)* is just the constant expression of the potential of the origin. The origin is always the potential which I have to fulfil, but it is a potential as a reality not just as a concept or idea. As soon as there is the beginning of a process, there is a necessity to follow that process. The ideal is to follow it spontaneously. There is a famous quotation from Hegel in which he states that freedom is present necessity. That is very Daoist!

Question: Is there ever a specific link made between the yuan (元) and the jing (精), essences?

Not in this text. Later on there are a lot. The Neijing also makes a link with the essences via the kidneys. If the kidneys store the essences and are responsible for providing all the essences in the body these are not only the essences of the kidneys, for example bone marrow, or those for the production of liquids and blood, but they are also to make the seed of life. The seed of life is present in the sperm and blood to produce another life. Later texts give more specific explanations.

THE ROLE OF THE STOMACH

Lingshu chapter 60 says:

'The stomach is the sea of *qi* and blood coming from the liquids and grains. The clouds and *qi* (*yun qi* 雲 氣) which come from this sea circulate everywhere under heaven. *Qi* and blood that come from the stomach form the trenches (tunnels) of the meridians (*jing sui* 經 隧).'

Here we have a vision of the *qi* of the stomach sustaining the renewal of *yin* and *yang*, nutriment and defence, and blood and *qi*. This is at the very basis of what in later texts is called posterior heaven. If the *qi* of the stomach is insufficient, for example due to starvation, the *qi* of the whole body is soon unbalanced. We see in Suwen chapter 18:

'The normal *qi* of a well-balanced man (he who follows the norm of life) is received from the stomach. The stomach is the normal *qi* of a well-balanced man. When a man no longer has the *qi* of the stomach then it is called counter-current (*ni* 逆) and this counter-current is death.'

The three trenches

Lingshu chapter 71:

'When the grains enter the stomach, they divide into three trenches (*san sui* 三 隧), residues and waste (*zao po* 糟 粕), body fluids (*jin ye* 津 液), and ancestral *qi* (*zong qi* 宗 氣).'

This passage has the same character, *sui* (隧), as we saw for the trenches of the meridians in Lingshu chapter 16. The image is of a trench with a lot of circulation. A modern analogy would be a large pipe underneath the street containing all the other pipes for gas and electricity and so on. A lot of circulation is contained within a protected area. We find this expression *sui* used for the twelve meridians because they are twelve kinds of trenches used by all sorts of circulations. The three trenches coming from the stomach mentioned in Lingshu chapter 71 do not represent something physical, but indicate that from the work of the stomach there are three ways of circulating because there are three kinds of form: the residues and waste (*zao po* 糟 粕), the body fluids (*jin ye* 津 液) and ancestral *qi* (*zong qi* 宗 氣).

These three represent one kind of circulation for each level of the triple heater. What is heavy and thick will descend and become the residues and waste which are processed by the lower heater. The bodily liquids, *jin ye* (津 液), which are linked with the middle heater, are used for the renewal of the form, and the *zong qi* (宗氣), located in the sea of *qi* in the upper heater, is for all the *qi* without form and which rises upwards.

THE TRIPLE HEATER AND ZONG QI

The text of Lingshu chapter 71 continues by presenting three kinds of *qi*, ancestral, constructive and defensive. There is a first division into three and then a second division into three related to the three levels of the triple heater and the stomach in the centre. The triple heater represents the triple aspect of the life-giving *qi*.

'The ancestral *qi* accumulates in the middle of the chest (*xiong zhong* 胸 中). It goes out at the larynx, passing the vital circulations of the heart and makes inhalation and exhalation function.'

The character for accumulation, *ji* (積), is the same as we saw earlier in Lingshu chapter 75. Here the *qi* is accumulated in the stomach to allow the circulation of nutrition and defence. There is no congestion of *qi* or blockage. If *qi* accumulates without circulation there will be a blockage. In Lingshu chapter 71 all the *qi* converging in the middle of the chest is disseminated and circulates like clouds spreading everywhere under heaven.

The *qi* is attracted by the middle of the chest, attracted by its position in the upper part of the body, just as the *sui* (隧) always attract water. Water accumulates in the sea, but the sea never overflows. As water is accumulated it evaporates in the form of clouds and mist, so nothing is blocked and everything remains in its place. *Qi* is constantly attracted but if it follows its natural movement it goes upwards. Water, following its own natural movement, goes downwards, to the sea, which is in the lowest position.

The *qi* naturally goes to the upper heater, to the sea of *qi* in the middle of the chest, and appears at the level of the larynx. It passes through the circulations of the heart in order to make exhalation and inhalation work well. This is the presentation of *zong qi* in Lingshu chapter 71.

The beating of the heart is also linked to the *zong qi* in Suwen chapter 18. The heart and its circulation ensures a regular movement of blood and *qi* which can be felt at the pulse. It is very clear that what is called *zong qi* is that which gives the rhythm for all circulation. It is the merging of all *qi* and if it merges well it is in balance. If the balance is correct the rhythm will also be correct, and respiration will be regular and full. It is the same for the beating of the heart and the movement of life through the blood and *qi* of the whole body. All of this relies on *zong qi*.

The character *zong* (宗) is made with the image of a roof of a building at the top, and below the influence emanating from the ancestors and descending upon the offspring *shi* (示). In the classical interpretation of the character from the second century AD, the three vertical lines were interpreted as the manifestation of a triple form of what is above, for instance the sun, the moon and the planets (cf Wieger's Chinese Characters Lesson 3D). Specifically in this character they represent all the spiritual influences coming from heaven.

This element (示) forms part of the character for spirits, *shen* (神), and part of many other characters meaning sacrifice, or that which comes from heaven as blessings. What is hidden in heaven is descending to earth with the sun, the moon and the planets as a triple manifestation.

Influences descending from heaven suggest the first meaning of the character *zong* (宗), which was a temple for ancestor worship. This was the place where family members gathered together to perform rituals to help the ancestors, and to receive blessings and inspiration from them. The rituals ensured the continuity of the life of the lineage. So we can understand why the character *zong* also has the meaning of ancestors, or the continuity of the ancestors.

During their lifetime a Chinese person can have a lot of names, a birth name, nicknames, names given by friends or by themselves when something changes in their life, but after death they are given a posthumous name, particularly they are the emperor. If you look at the list of posthumous names of emperors you will often find the character *zong*, but never for the first emperor of a dynasty. *Zong* is only used for the continuity of the line. It also has the meaning of an important gathering because it is the gathering of all the members of a family, along with all the deceased members too.

Through *zong* we understand how we have to be faithful to the origin, how to ensure the continuity and the expression of that. Just by understanding this character in Chinese we can realize the potential of the origin through *zong qi*. It is the blending of all kinds of *qi* in order to make a good rhythm and balance of harmony in blood and *qi*, *yin* and *yang* and so on. If you translate *zong* by 'gathering' it is not enough, if you translate it by 'ancestral' there can be a lot of misunderstanding. There is really no absolutely true translation. In English and French we simply do not have the same concept, so we must go through the Chinese meaning in order to understand.

DA QI

The relationship with respiration, with food and the stomach is all presented in the text of Lingshu chapter 71 as we saw previously. In Lingshu chapter 56 there is a sentence which expresses similar ideas, however, it does not refer to *zong qi* but to *da qi* (大 氣):

> 'The great *qi* (*da qi* 大 氣) which beat without circulating, accumulate in the middle of the chest (*xiong zhong* 胸 中); the name is sea of *qi* (*qi hai* 氣 海).'

This is the same idea as the beating of life with the moving *qi* in the chest. You can see the movement in the beating of the heart. When it circulates it takes other names: blood and *qi*, nutrition and defence, or whatever else. It does not take the name of *zong qi*.

YING QI

The character *ying* (營) is very simple. It has the fire character (*huo* 火) twice at the top. To have two fires side by side like this is different from having them one on top of the other, which would indicate too much fire, or an intense burning. Fire next to fire suggests a gentle fire, acting as life-giving warmth and light, and providing the means for cooking. Underneath this is a depiction of something which is usually understood as a fence around a village or a military encampment (呂) (cf Wieger's Chinese Characters Lesson 90G). Inside the encampment is a representation of barracks or tents.

This is the depiction of a basic settlement, a village with everything necessary for life, or the organization of a military camp with everything in the right place and order. *Ying* is often used in classical texts. We have seen it in relation to earthly organization, in parallel with the character *jing* (經), the character for the meridians which reflect heavenly organization.

Ying is the building up and completion of something, an organization to ensure the achievement of a goal. *Ying* means to organise, to manage and express something, to nourish something with the meaning of caring for it and enabling it to express this organization. After this there is the maintenance of that organization, and the ability to take care of all aspects of its life, not only in terms of food but also of on-going repairs. So a translation of *ying* by 'nutrition' is not exactly bad but is not enough. It is too narrow because *ying* is more than to nourish. It means to take care of all the earthly, *yin* aspects of life inside the body: to build, to repair, to maintain, to nourish, to act in such a way that all the substances and essences are transported to the right place where they can be used for their specific purpose.

Lingshu chapter 71 says:

The *ying qi* produces the body fluids by secretion. It pours into the vital circulations, it makes the blood by transformation. It gives splendour and prosperity (*rong* 榮) to the four extremities (limbs). Inside it pours into the five *zang* and six *fu*, and it corresponds to the laws of the passing of time (*ke shu* 刻 數).'

This means that we have relationships between the *ying* and the body fluids, *jin ye* (津 液), as if the *jin ye* were a kind of secretion from the *ying qi*. The *ying qi* covers everything the *qi* is able to do when it transports and transforms in order to maintain the body form, liquids and flesh and so on. It embraces all the activities of *qi* leading to the use of any form of the essences.

The *ying qi* are related to the body fluids because part of the body fluids, specifically the *ye* (液), maintain the form, bring nourishment and so on. Both are linked with the spleen and stomach, and with the middle heater in coming from the assimilation of essences at that level, but they are not equivalent. When we speak of *ying* we speak of all these general activities. When we speak of body fluids we speak of very specific body functions which are not only for maintenance or nutrition but are also closely linked with defensive *qi*. The *jin* (津) are more closely linked with defensive *qi* and with all the effects of clearing, cleansing and refreshing. All these functions are closer to defensive *qi* than constructive, nutritive *qi*.

Because they have a substance and form, the *jin* (津) are the result of the work of the *qi* in the middle heater.

They also have relationships with the vital circulation, specifically blood and *qi*. The relationship with blood is made through transformation. Blood is not a body fluid as such, but it comes from the activity of *qi* natural to the middle heater, and at the level of the spleen and stomach, expressing the capacity to build, rebuild and maintain. Blood has the function of nourishing and maintaining, but it is not the same as *ying qi*. Perception and knowledge, spirits and consciousness are stored in the blood, which is not the case for *ying qi*.

The *mai* (脈) are the vital circulation of all the fluids and blood in the body, and there is a strong presence of *ying qi* within the *mai*. The *ying qi* deals with what is heavy and full, the *yin*, and has to follow some kind of path and be pushed by the impulse of the vital circulation, just as the blood circulates. The image often given in texts is that of the movement of an army. The head chariot or tank and the bulk of the men and equipment travel on the road while various scouts, not carrying heavy equipment, move around at a distance from them, but they need to come back to the main part of the army for food and supplies. This is the relationship between the nutrition and defence and the vital circulation (*mai* 脈), and why the *ying qi* is said to circulate through *mai* and the *wei qi* outside the *mai*. But reconstruction is at work everywhere within the body, within the skin, at the level of the body hair and so on. It also works in the depths of the flesh where there is much to rebuild and maintain. Defensive *qi* is felt everywhere, at the surface and in the depths.

The character used for bringing splendour is *rong* (榮). The upper part is exactly the same as in the character *ying* (火火), but underneath instead of a barracks there is a tree (木) representing vegetation. The meaning of *rong* (榮) is that when everything is well maintained and nourished, there is a prosperity given to life, and this is visible on the exterior as a kind of splendour. When the sap is circulating well in a tree and you can see it in the colour of the leaves and in the consistency of the branches. *Rong* can be used in medical texts to mean the external sign of good maintenance inside the body. The five *zang* and six *fu* represent all the various functions of the body fluids and nutriments - everything which makes the substance necessary for the good functioning of the organism.

That the *ying qi* 'corresponds to the laws of the passing of time' is just to say that it circulates through the vital circulation (*mai* 脈) in the body, according to the rhythm given by the *zong qi* (宗 氣) and by the beating of the heart. And that inner rhythm is constant day and night. Our hearts beat with nearly the same rate during the day as during the night and it is the same for respiration. Therefore in this very short text in Chinese we have the essence of *ying qi*.

WEI QI

The character *wei* (衛) is easy to explain because it is made with *xing* (行), to circulate, to move, or to walk, which is the character translated as 'element' in the five elements. It gives the idea of a motion which is very regular, with a nice alternation of *yin* and *yang*. It is as regular as the course of the planets or the sun and moon and is a character which is used for the movement of the heavenly bodies. In the middle is one of the characters for leather; not the rough animal hide itself, but the hide when it has been worked to make something. It is used to give warriors protection, so immediately there is the idea of something which protects. *Wei* therefore depicts a regular motion and the protection provided by leather, and is the defence, the guard around the palace or the protection around something. We see in Lingshu chapter 71:

'The *wei qi* comes out with the rapidity and eagerness of brave *qi*. This circulation takes place first in the four limbs, and especially where there is a separation between the flesh (*fen rou* 分 肉), between the layers of skin, without stopping.'

These are the qualities which we always find in descriptions of defensive *qi*. The idea of something warrior-like underlies it. The bravery and ability to move forward is the *yang* movement. This is the contrary of *ying qi* because it does not circulate under the impulse given by the *mai*, the vital circulation, but is itself full of eager strength and being *yang* is able to circulate by itself. It is not in charge of transporting nutriments, and being formless it can circulate through even the most imperceptible crevasse or crack in the body. We can understand *fen rou* (分 肉) as the place where there is a split or separation in the flesh, from the large valleys to the invisible places inside the mass of the flesh. We know from other texts that there is no mass or bulk which is not completely pervaded by a multitude of unlimited circulations. The *qi* pervades everything, and here it is *yang* in nature. Lingshu chapter 71 continues:

'In the day it circulates in the *yang* and in the night it circulates in the *yin.*'

The *yang* force is everything which is linked by the *yang* and represented by the *yang* meridians, by *yang* activities and muscular movement, and by the opening of the sense organs. During the night it circulates in the *yin* represented by the *yin* organs, the five *zang.* This is when we are at rest, not moving our limbs, and not orienting our sense organs towards the exterior. During the day it circulates in the *yang* and enables us to be directed towards the outside. During the night it goes to the *yin* to regenerate itself. The comparison with the sun is important because during the night the sun regenerates itself in order to be ready for the next morning. The sun's mother takes care of him on the other side of the earth! This is exactly the same metaphor used for *wei qi*. During the night it has to be regenerated, just as we saw earlier with the scouts or soldiers who have to come back to their barracks to eat. Otherwise they will be lost and killed.

The details of the circulation of *wei qi* are also found in Lingshu chapter 76. It always starts with the kidneys and follows the *ke* (剋) cycle: kidneys, heart, lung, liver and spleen. It is always by the proper circulation of the *shao yang* (少 陽) of the foot that the *wei qi* circulates in the five *zang* and six *fu*. It is always by means of the kidneys that it circulates in the depths during the night. This link with the kidneys is very important for the defensive *qi*. We will see more of this by looking at Lingshu chapter 18:

> 'Man receives the *qi* from grains. The grains enter the stomach to be transmitted to the lung. The five *zang* and six *fu* will all receive this *qi*. What is clear (*qing* 清) produces the *ying*, what is unclear (*zhuo* 濁) produces the *wei*.'

This is within the specific context of the digestion because the grains are the starting point. In the process of digestion that which is assimilated first is called clear, and in this context that is the *ying*. That which is unclear descends to the lower abdomen and lower heater, and this goes on to form the *wei qi* coming from the lower heater.

> 'The constructive *ying qi* circulates within the vital circulations (*mai* 脈). The defensive *wei qi* circulates outside the vital circulations. The constructive *qi* runs its circuit without stopping 50 times and is once again the big reunion (*da hui* 大 會). *Yin* and *yang* interlink and interconnect like a ring without end.'

So when the *qi* is with the *yang* there is activity, and when the *qi* is with the *yin* there is rest. Further on Lingshu chapter 18 states:

> 'That which nourishes (*ying*) comes out of the middle heater. That which defends (*wei*) comes out of the lower heater (or according to certain texts the upper heater).'

Here there is an obvious relationship between the unclear *qi* and the lower heater. But if there is a relationship with the lower heater there is also a relationship with the kidneys, specifically through the *shao yin* (少 陰) of the foot. From this we know what gives this essential *qi* its *yang* quality. The best of the essences are used to nourish and maintain the body through the nutriments and fluids and also by the blood.

What remains, because it has a kind of strength given by the process of digestion and assimilation, renews the forces of *qi*, and is able to give to this *qi* the very *yang* quality which is something related to the lower heater, the kidneys and the *shao yin*. It is certainly related to the *yang* of the kidneys or to the fire of the lower heater. This is the fire within the *yin*, *ming men* (命 門), the authentic *yang*. It is through this that the *wei qi*, with its strength coming from nutrition, is able to make its defence, obeying the rhythm of life, and expressing the *yang* power at its source in the kidneys and the lower heater. In the same way the constructive and maintaining *ying qi* expresses the nourishing power of the earth and the ability to give form, being sustained by the kidneys and the gentle fire of the *yang* of the kidneys in order to be able to make all the forms of life. This is on the *yang* side because we need to have this relationship with the origin as well. The *wei qi* therefore also expresses the fire, or *yang*, of the origin through what is assimilated by the digestion.

It is through the lower heater and specifically the *yang* of the lower heater that the *wei qi* takes its *yang* power. The *wei qi* circulates through the chest and the upper sea of *qi*, and is able to circulate through the upper heater. From the upper heater comes the *wei qi* and whatever else is circulated by the *qi*: the *ying*, the blood and the body fluids. So we know that the *wei qi*, with its special effect on the outer layers of the skin, has a double link which is also described in Lingshu chapter 18, a link with *tai yang* (太 陽), the bladder meridian, with the lower heater and the water element, and the *yang* of the kidneys. The defensive *qi* has a lot to do with *tai yang*. This is developed in the Shang han lun and its school.

The defensive *qi* also has a relationship with the lung and the skin. It is linked with the movement of the lung and the spreading out of *qi* by the lung up to the periphery of the body and the outer layers of skin. This is not a contradiction. We have to see that it must be linked with the origin in order for the strength given by food to become defensive *qi*, just as there is also a link with the lung and its *qi* in order to propel it outward to the furthest layers of the skin. Both nutrition and defence are part of what is in the *zong qi*, and what is distributed with the good rhythm given by the *zong qi*.

QI AS MIST AND DEW

Finally there is a description of *qi* given in Lingshu chapter 30:

'The upper heater spreads and propagates the

tastes of the five grains. It invades the skin like smoke; it gives power and strength to the body and moisture to the body hair. It is like mist (*wu* 霧) and dew (*lu* 露). That is called *qi*.'

Here the *qi is* spreading from the sea of *qi* in the upper heater, diffusing the essences coming from food, and permeating the skin like smoke. It gives the *yang* aspects of power and strength to the body, and moisture, the *yin* aspect, to the body hair. Mist is a kind of vapour which is nearly water, and dew is water which is nearly *qi*. This is a very good definition of the circulation from the upper heater.

We can categorize *yin yang qi* as nutrition/ maintenance and defence, blood and *qi*, or essences and *qi*. They are different but they are also intermingled, and they must be in balance. Whenever there is an imbalance this is the beginning of a process which leads to disease.

1NDEX

ENGLISH LANGUAGE REFERENCES

Roger Ames, *Sun Tzu, The Art of War,* Ballantine Books 1993

Charles le Blanc, *Huai Nan Tzu: Philosophical Synthesis in Early Han Thought*, Hong Kong University Press, 1985

John Knowblock and Jeffrey Riegel, *The Annals of Lü Buwei,* Stanford University Press 2000

John Knowblock, *Xunzi Art of War,* Hunan People's Publishing House, China

D.C. Lau, *Mencius,* Chinese University Press, Hong Kong 2003

D.C. Lau and Roger Ames, *Yuan Dao, Tracing the Dao to its Source,* (Huainanzi chapter 1) Ballantine Books, New York, 1998

James Legge, *The Chinese Classics,* SMC Publishing Inc. Taipei

James Legge, *The Texts of Taoism,* Dover Publications, New York

Burton Watson, *Chuang Tzu,* Columbia University Press, New York, 1964